A DOUBLE LIFE

A Double Life

In Poetry

&

Translation

by

STUART FRIEBERT

Pinyon Publishing
Montrose, CO

Cover and Interior Eagle Photographs by Steve Friebert

Photograph of Stuart Friebert and James Joyce's statue by Diane Vreuls

Design by Susan Entsminger

First Edition: October 2019

Pinyon Publishing
23847 V66 Trail, Montrose, CO 81403
www.pinyon-publishing.com

Library of Congress Control Number: 2019949138
ISBN: 978-1-936671-58-8

Acknowledgments

Great thanks to the following publications, in which many of these words have previously appeared:

The Antioch Review

Copper Nickel

The Font – A Literary Journal for Language Teachers

Great River Review

in den rissen der zeit ("poesia 4" / scaneg Verlag / Munich / 2018)

Offcourse

Pinyon Review

Plume

Trans-Lit/2

Translation Review

Voyages

World Literature Today

The Grass and Domin accounts owe a great deal to David Young, whose friendship & acuity over some sixty years I treasure beyond measure.

In Loving Memory of Gary Entsminger,
Poet-Pal & Editor/Publisher extraordinaire,
without WHOM …

& with Great Thanks to Susan Entsminger
for her editing & design magic as well

≈

And in Memory of
Hilde Domin
Tankred Dorst
Günter Grass
Calvin Hernton
Miroslav Holub
Martin Joos
Michael Mann
Giovanni Raboni
Alfredo Rizzardi
Vinio Rossi
Marin Sorescu
Zigurds Zile

≈

CONFIDENCE
In Salonica
I know someone who reads me,
and in Bad Nauheim.
That's already two.
—Günter Eich

Contents

Early Encounters

"Were you in the Military?" Remembering Zigurds Zile

I

"IF so," the Great Clips stylist said, "we can offer you a dollar discount, thanks to new management's generosity!" Last time she cut my hair I'd have said a quick *no*, but my pal who survived Vietnam recently convinced me otherwise. True, for all five years while pursuing graduate degrees at the University of Wisconsin in the 50s, I'd enlisted in the reserves, but resigned in 1958 when I began teaching. My fluency in German had gotten me assigned to MI, i.e. a military intelligence unit, but that hardly constituted 'serving' in my mind.

"Hell, they could have shipped you out somewhere scary at any time," Blake grinned and saluted. "Besides," he went on, "they also serve who watch dumb films about how to crack safes, or threaten prisoners to get them to cough up useful info." After knocking back a few too many brews at his go-to Bar & Grill joint down the road, I'd blab about the mindless meetings we reservists were required to attend, capped by the requisite two weeks getting our butts drilled off summers at various army camps.

"Tell me again," Blake poked me when we ran out of other chat, "did you really get left standing alone when your unit to a man all got their sharpshooter medals?" Not about to cut to the chase, I ordered us another round, gently spun him around

3

on the shabby stool, and retold the whole tale for the last time, I promised myself, of that Fort Leonard Wood summer. We first observed a moment of silence in honor of General Wood, a hero to Blake and me. Wood had commanded the Rough Riders during the Spanish-American War and went on to win the first four ballots in the election to replace Teddy Roosevelt before Harding was nominated instead. "Here's to Lenny," we crooned, banging our beer cans together till the bartender wagged a finger.

2

A law student at Wisconsin, Zig, as he liked to go by, was older and wiser than the rest of us lowlifes in the MI unit. Atop a bear of a body, his head seemed able to swivel around in a circle so you couldn't get away with much. If you did mess up, put the unit at some risk—one's mistakes became everyone's in the eyes of most officers—Zig would take you aside, flash a wicked smile, stick his tongue in the space between his front teeth, and rattle off curses in Latvian. Then he'd hand you a little pocket dictionary in case you were curious about what he'd called your mother.

At Master Sergeant he was several ranks above us, and something of an aide to the lieutenant who presided over our monthly meetings. Gently keeping us in line for the most part, Zig had to remind us at times that it was a privilege to serve any which way. "If you'd been born in Riga, and spent your wet-behind-the-ears years worrying about the Russians, then the Germans, then the Russians again, you'd keep the grumbling to a minimum," he'd say when we got on his nerves. "Try to stop feeling so god-damn superior," he'd resort to when our whining waxed.

Monthly meetings at the armory, presided over by the lieutenant who was finishing a PhD in linguistics, usually found us watching some ERPI film the army hoped would prepare us for duty in the clandestine lane. At times we were assigned roles as prisoner and interrogator, which put an end to the yawning. When Zig played prisoner, given his early life behind enemy lines, we really shaped and sharpened up. A joker at times, Zig concealed a huge luger he'd carved out of basswood and drew at a testy moment. Even the lieutenant ducked. At Christmas Zig gifted us with little crèche animals he'd fashioned from the gun.

3

When orders arrived to report to Ft. Leonard Wood in Missouri for our two-week stint of duty the summer of 1954, Zig offered to get us there in his jalopy. When he said we'd share the minimal expenses equally, hence could bank the rest of the travel allowance, three of us readily agreed. The other guys in the unit went by Greyhound bus, stopping off en route to see family here and there.

Researching the roads to Missouri, Zig decided we'd need at least two days to get there in time, absent any jalopy problems. "Set your watches, grunts, we're leaving 6 AM sharp two days after the semester ends." Knowing I was courting a gal hard and would take off to her rental any break I had—she'd taken a job waitressing in Madison for the summer—he clowned, "Be sure to give her a sweaty kiss from me when you sneak into her digs at 5:30. Be late, though, and you'll get your own sorry self to Missouri or be court-martialed."

Madison was already heating up over 90, but we soon hit 100 degrees halfway down Illinois, when to save more of the travel allowance Zig decided to bed us down in a cornfield on a side road off the main highway. I can still sense the tip of the farmer's twelve-gauge, his dog growling at his side, when he prodded us awake. "Don't mind you boys squatting here for the night, ain't planted no seeds yet; but I sure as heck don't appreciate your vehicle digging me some ruts I don't need." When he pointed to Zig's jalopy we'd tried to get clear off the road, his dog broke free and circled it, barking his head off. When Zig plucked a dollar bill out of his wallet, the farmer cut him off. "Hell, kid, you look like you need that more than me. Just vacate the premises now," he said with a half-smile.

4

Arriving half exhausted, we were shown to our bunks in something of a Quonset hut, the air filled with dust motes. The sarge who'd be our minder flipped a quarter onto a sheet tightly tucked into the wooden frame. "No bounce no extra kitchen detail, unless you love peeling taters," he growled. Zig led us in a snappy salute, and off we trotted behind the sarge to our typewriter stations in central HQ. A stack of documents awaited us at each, and aside from pre-breakfast field drills, we spent the whole time poring over documents purported to have been retrieved from captured WW II German files and assorted recording-keeping books.

"Gentlemen, your job is to translate as many as quickly as possible as we are still building a case for any future legal action to be taken in the matter of war crimes," the lieutenant in charge intoned with some gravity. He also swore us to secrecy "for the foreseeable future." The way the brain erases most of a night's tumbling images, I soon forgot what I'd only just been feverishly involved translating the day before and no longer recall anything I read.

A few days before our tour was over, we were surprised to get a directive to report to the firing-range for "weapons training." Zig thought there must be some mistake—other units from around the country were also assembled at the fort—and went up the chain on our behalf to a captain's office. He'd never come by to review us, but we'd been informed he was responsible for everything and everyone in MI that summer. Rumor had it he was a high school principal from Minneapolis, said to conduct assemblies with a baton, and loved pretending he was Dimitri Mitropoulis, then conductor of the Minneapolis Symphony Orchestra. "Yep," Zig shrugged, "means us, too. Something about every soldier must know from guns and bullets. Should have brought some ear plugs."

My father, to his great disappointment, hadn't been able to teach me how to shoot his beloved twelve-gauge shotgun. I'd learned to take it apart, reassemble it properly, clean and oil it religiously, but that didn't suffice. In something of a funk, I lagged behind the rest of our unit marching to the range till Zig looked back and pumped his fist. Demerits would cost us all.

Serious heat had us all soaking our shirts the first hour, when the sarge was finally satisfied we knew the front end from the stock of the M1 carbine we'd be using to hit the circular targets a hundred yards down range. Huge, bale-like doughnuts of straw, their surface was painted in bright red concentric rings leading to the tiny bull's-eye. "Now listen up," the sarge went on, "you will see a small circular green sign raised on a stick from a trench immediately below the target. It will move around to show you where, if at all, your rounds hit anywhere on the target. Under no circumstances should the next man down the line fire away until the indicator disappears. There is a human hand at the bottom of the stick, understood?" We all nodded in unison.

Stationed next to me, Zig whispered, "Just squat your eyes, it'll keep the sun to a minimum." After we finished our rounds, guys down the line from us were ordered to start shooting next. Making small talk while waiting for them to exhaust their rounds, we were suddenly jolted by a scream coming downwind from the trench at the target site, whereupon a loud chorus of whistles silenced the whole firing line. Hustled along in ragged formation, we were ordered to make double time back to our barracks. Rumors abounding, it wasn't till the morning's drill review that the captain finally stood before us, tersely reading from a bulletin, his hand clearly shaking.

All I recall him announcing was that someone, to our great relief not in our unit, had fired before the little green sign disappeared. The human hand raising the stick had strayed above the sight line and it was shredded so badly it had to be amputated. All talk was hushed from that moment on till the closing ceremony two days later. The captain finished his remarks—how proud he was of all his troops, how fortunate we were to be Americans in the land of the free, blah blah and more blah—before reading off names of all who'd won a sharpshooting medal. "If I've read your name, step forward now!" he bellowed, pointing to us.

In the middle of the bridge over the Mississippi on our way back, Zig elbowed me in the side. "You'll not soon forget the honor you brought to our unit. The only one not to have earned the SS, way to go, man!"

Down on His Knees: Remembering Martin Joos

IN 1953, if you knocked on his door during office hours, he'd sweep you in with a huge wave, then grab his old alarm clock, something of a crazy antique, ask you how much time you could afford, set the alarm accordingly, and once you stammered out your question, proceed to surround it with so much information, buttressed by graphs, charts, tomes from the recesses of his library behind him, that your poor question almost cried for help.

But how fortunate we were, graduate students in German in Madison at UW, to come under, as well as before, one could say, his tutelage, which often morphed into a spell. Phonetics and Middle & Old High German were my tunnels into his inner kingdom. His throne was an oversized armchair he'd not sit in for long in the dusky classroom in Bascom Hall, because he'd leap up again and again, now to the blackboard to chalk an enormous sagittal section of a human head, now to slide on his knees to a stop right before anyone who'd not yet learned not to sit in the front row.

At the board, he'd X spots within the mouth's cavity to indicate where this or that sound emanated from, punctuated — we eventually learned to take more careful notes when he did — by slowly intoned remarks; e.g. "German is far less guttural than English! Take the word 'ball,' which you all say way back here" —

another, smaller X chalked at the end of the tongue — "while every German spits it out from the tongue's tip" — a slightly larger X chalked right behind the lips.

Down on his knees beside the "volunteer" in the front row, he'd tilt her head, gently pry open her mouth, then ask her to demonstrate both pronunciations, often followed by an "observation," he liked to call it, that even from her single pronunciation of "ball" he could tell where she grew up as a child, as well as where she subsequently moved to, i.e. was exposed to different manners of pronunciation "she couldn't help but be influenced by!"

Who could ever forget his typical exam queries: "Speaker said 'butter cup,' listener heard 'butter up': EXPLAIN, and accompany if necessary with skillful illustrations." Or a favorite, which I've often leaned on in my teaching: "Wolfram von Eschenbach's EYE & EAR!"

2

Thanks to Prof. Joos' offhand suggestion, that graduate students develop a beginning German program for grade schoolers, to be taught summers, two women and I submitted a curriculum plan that was approved. So there we were that next summer, under the supervision of Joos, signing up some twenty children, among them his own daughter. Talk about upping the ante! Our fright at first never quite dissipating, we somehow managed to earn generally good marks from him about how we handled matters. At the party celebrating the course's first summer, my fellow instructors overheard Joos saying to a visiting colleague, whose son was interested in enrolling the next time around, "Young Friebert, whose German is not at all contemptible, will likely continue instructing next summer, and inasmuch as his fellows are graduating, we'll find substitutes."

I've long worn that appraisal as a badge of honor …

3

Although of course we students were quite curious about the histories of our professors, without Google and today's resources we rarely found out "stuff" to pass around. There were the inevitable rumors, especially about Joos. It was widely known he'd served as a cryptologist during WW II, and was said to have helped crack a Japanese code at some point. The War Department awarded him a Distinguished Service Citation for having helped develop "communication systems." At one point he let slip that he studied engineering "when I was your age." He did have some sort of machine in his office that I think he called a "sound spectograph," into which he'd occasionally ask you to say a simple word like "yes" then fiddle with the dials and print out a graph of your "signature shape." He'd tear it off the roll and give it to you. I wish I'd had the good sense to have saved it, not to mention have him autograph it as well …

4

You knew you'd made it to graduate school heaven if he ever invited you to play chess with him in his office, which he did one late afternoon when we'd finished grading exams of the beginning German courses we TAs taught. Winking he was fresh out of rum to "spot it," he made me a cup of tea in a mug he must never have washed, because its insides were dark brown, held out both hands, a pawn concealed in each, and said "Choose your color." Out came black, he pushed the queen's pawn two spaces and yawned, as he usually did after every class, come to think. All else I now recall, some sixty-five years later, is it only took him just twenty or so moves to whisper "Schachmatt, junger Mann."

His Hand Went Slowly Up: Remembering Michael Mann

I

MY tail between my legs, having been let go in the second year of my first three-year teaching contract, I headed to the Modern Language Association in the winter of 1958-59 quite depressed. Interviewing for a new job, along with hundreds of others at the yearly MLA meeting on the fringes of all the proceedings and programs, was an angst-laden prospect even if one left behind a decent record, not to mention having published at least something in a reputable journal as well. Add more angst for not, in those days, being able to access letters of recommendation one was obliged to have on file.

While I was fortunate to have lined up an interview with Harvard, I knew they needed to cast a wide net given their growing needs—German language and literature were still a healthy draw in those days, though Russian and Slavic studies were coming on strong.

If I'd been more alert, I might have sensed there was more to the question of whether or not I'd be prepared to teach an upper-level course on Hesse, Kafka, and Mann, having mostly concentrated on 18th and 19th century writers. Henry Hatfield, then chair, I knew had written what many considered an important book on Thomas Mann, and was said to have been a friend of the Mann family as well. He wondered whether or not I'd be intimidated by heady graduate students, as the course

13

would be open to them as well as upper-level undergraduate majors. While I knew I'd be in for a long summer of preparing, inasmuch as I'd really only read Hesse carefully, but Kafka only somewhat, and Mann hardly at all, I said I didn't think so; but so nervously I felt sure that would soon be that. However, Hatfield and Stuart Atkins, his interviewing partner, suddenly veered off into German, clearly to test my oral skills. Inasmuch as I'd also spent some fifteen months studying in Germany, as one of the first American exchange students after WW II, I soon had them nodding to each other, and they quickly broke the interview off. However, I left feeling pretty sure I'd not meet Harvard standards even for an entry-level position, given what I suspected were troubling letters of recommendation from Mt. Holyoke staff.

When spring came along, and Professor Hatfield called to offer me a position as instructor in German, I shook, lost my voice a moment, and stumbled to a chair.[1] After reassuring himself I was all right, he quickly added that I'd be among a group of some five or six other souls, only one or two of whom could expect to be promoted at the end of our three-year contract. Oh, oh, here we go again, I thought, and had the temerity to ask for a few days to think things through. Clearly, Prof. Hatfield was not used to being put off, hence curtly agreed. Having many times since wondered, as we all surely do, what course my life might have taken if I hadn't moved to Cambridge, I am certain that, along with that exchange year in Germany, no other event would have defined my working life as much.

2

So there I was, calling roll in the introductory session of

---

1 When Mt. Holyoke's president heard I'd managed to land at Harvard after having been let go, he congratulated me for winning a post-doc fellowship. Biting my tongue, I did not correct him.

what the students would call HKM—it was of course expected to be conducted in German—when one voice responding "anwesend" ("present") was clearly clipped as only a native would pronounce it. While I had quickly glanced up to try to connect faces to names, I paused, said "Michael Mann" again, and finally spotted a plump hand rising from the midst of some thirty students. His face, clearly twice as old as everyone else's, sporting a pronounced cleft chin, bore a slight smile, giving way to a chiseled countenance. When he also repeated "anwesend," I mumbled "schon gut, schon gut" (akin to "enough already"), taking a long moment to collect myself, when Michael Mann raised a white handkerchief atop a pencil and said, more softly, "Waffenruhe" ("truce"), which got us all laughing. As if that weren't enough to break the ice, a clever graduate student, who would prove to be intimidating all semester long, literally sang Kafka's "Ein Buch muß die Axt sein für das gefrorene Meer in uns" ("A book must be the axe for the frozen sea in us.").

We fairly breezed through Hesse, inasmuch as most of the students, it turned out, had already imbibed him along the way to shedding teenage skin, although I couldn't get them to take *Narziß und Goldmund* more seriously. Perhaps I was especially fond of it because a German classmate from my student days in Germany had somehow managed to get Hesse to inscribe it after a reading in a Swiss venue: "Dies ist wohl mein Buch!" "Wohl" is pure Hesse ("This is really/perhaps my book," given "wohl" has two basic, disparate meanings); and I'd made it central to the way I thought Hesse should be read. Though I encouraged free-wheeling discussion, mostly staying on the sidelines, just a handful of undergraduates engaged one another vigorously. The graduate students were strangely silent. In general, I found them less spirited than the undergraduates, perhaps having to do with the slog it often is to finish even an MA, let alone a PhD, in many a graduate program. In the last stretch to my PhD, not that long before teaching at Harvard, I sure felt the sap drying up …

Later, Michael, as I shall call him from now on, given our growing friendship, confirmed he stared out the window much of the time, as Hesse's prose rather bored him; struck him, as it did many an older reader, as too programmed, sentimental in unrevealing ways. Hesse's poems, however, were an entirely different matter. Michael had hoped we'd get around to including them as well. Alas, I wasn't as yet aware how fine they are, and it wasn't until James Wright and his son Franz co-translated a selection for Farrar, Straus & Giroux, that English readers got a sense of how much they'd been missing.

Michael had much more to offer when we got to Kafka; and shared what was perhaps an apocryphal tale of the time young Franz, left alone for a spell by his parents, managed to get his head stuck between the bars of the railing on the little balcony of their flat in Prague, said to want to watch life below on the square. When his parents returned, Franz was wailing. To calm him, his father thought to offer him some of his favorite chocolates, at which Franz wailed all the louder. That was the essence of all Kafka's characters' dilemmas, according to Michael. We joked it'd make a good exam question: Why would young Franz wail more loudly when …? A hint of an answer can be found in "The Hunger Artist"; i.e. he might have thought his father was trying to get him used to being caught between bars forever.

When we finally landed on Thomas Mann's shores during the last third of the semester, Michael suspected that I'd be so intimidated by his presence, not to mention his knowledge—I would have been!—that he worked out an agreement with Prof. Hatfield: absenting himself from my lectures and ensuing discussions, Michael would submit weekly five-page papers on the readings and confer with me privately. We would sometimes depart the campus in his car for a nearby "establishment," where we knocked back a brew or two and I mostly listened to parts of what would eventually become one of Michael's books, a biography of his father.

3

As the year wore on, and Michael was able, with permission, to quicken the path to his PhD, we drifted apart some, while rumors of how he came to be a doctoral student at Harvard began surfacing. The version I recall has Gret, his Swiss wife (nee Moser; 1916-2007), who'd been largely responsible for parenting their two young sons while Michael toured with the San Francisco Symphony as a violist, finally putting both her feet down, in response to which he decided he might well enjoy another career as a literary scholar given his background and exposure to literature. It was known that Thomas Mann's family's life — wife Katia's and their six children's — largely revolved around the paterfamilias's burgeoning career.

Less certain was the rumor that Michael had at first applied to Columbia, which turned him down, supposedly because of his age when applying, as something of a risky "investment"; whereupon Harvard, given Henry Hatfield's relationship with Thomas Mann, quickly smoothed the way to graduate-student status, and fast-tracked Michael to a PhD.

Michael caught me up on his progress after he asked me to testify to his character in court, along with others, as he'd been summoned to convince the court why it shouldn't revoke his driver's license: he had a habit of simply abandoning his car if he couldn't find a parking spot on his way to class, and the tickets had piled up. He treated us to a drink after the judge gave him "one more chance" to behave. The conversation quickly turned literary, and we learned that Michael joined forces with some faculty to form something of a literary gathering, modeled on Europe's salons. Meeting once a month, members were invited to talk about what they were working on, or read a paper. It's no exaggeration to say the evenings were often more exciting than anything we were up to in our daily doings.[2]

4

Near the end of the spring semester of my first year, Michael learned of my plans to marry in August and return in the fall for my second year of teaching as "an old married man," he teased. "I have a proposition for you: how would you and your mate like to sublet our apartment while we're off to Europe so I can finish my thesis?"[3] As I dimly recalled the layout for only having been there once or twice, he drew me a quick map to rush to my fiancée, who might not have agreed if she'd seen the place first, but that's another story ... He sweetened the deal by hinting there'd be "some bottles on a wall" we could "investigate."

While I could go on about the adventures the little apartment had in store for us, let me at least confirm there were indeed "bottles on a wall"; in fact, on a sturdy shelf directly above the couch in the living room; several dozen of them; and every single one an obviously expensive liqueur from all over the planet. What we won't also forget is opening a Fibber McGee-like closet, out of which tumbled great numbers of photographs that had not yet been organized in albums. We put a temporary end to

---

2   I've written elsewhere of my gratitude to Michael Mann for getting me to take my own German poems, which I'd begun writing while studying in Germany, much more seriously. Though we decided the batch I showed him in those "salon" days wouldn't be quite appropriate to introduce at a session, he worked with me on several, which eventually led to my being able to finish *Kein Wasser*, the first of my four collections in German.

3   A superb violist himself, Michael drew on his fount of knowledge and expertise to develop the thesis into a splendid book on Heinrich Heine's music criticism.

moving in, relieved the shelf of at least one bottle, spread out on the floor like kindergartners, and made our way through years of the Mann family's doings. At times I yelped, because I'd also been, for instance, to Kilchberg on Lake Zürich, where the family spent joyous times. Drunk on the sometimes intimate images, as well as feeling more and more guilty for such an intrusion, we tried, finally, stacking the photographs back as we'd remembered seeing them at first; and we never opened that closet again.

5

I never saw Michael again. He hadn't returned from working on his thesis by the time I'd seen the writing on the wall. Even with one year left on my contract, I sensed I wouldn't likely be promoted at Harvard. I simply hadn't published up to expectations; and having no other articles, much less a book, hatching away, I jumped at the offer of an assistant professorship at Oberlin, dashed off a note to Michael with our last month's rent, and we left for Ohio in late summer, 1961.

Given the difficult inter-faculty relationships in Oberlin's German Department, my first few years were hard sledding for us all. So when three years in I suddenly got a letter from Prof. Heinz Politzer, offering me a job at UC Berkeley, in which he mentioned a colleague would be Michael Mann, who sent me greetings, I was facing another watershed moment in my professional, as well as my family's personal, life. Funnily enough, I'd actually been hired to fill the vacancy in German Politzer had left at Oberlin, where he'd quickly become hugely popular, filling lecture halls, attracting students from across the literature spectrum to the courses he also offered in English. Especially "exciting," I'd heard from many students he'd attracted to German literature, were his lectures on Kafka. Hence it was no surprise that his book, *Franz Kafka: Parable and Paradox*, became something of a bestseller when it appeared in 1966.

Inasmuch as Berkeley's German Department was looking for someone with expertise in the 18th and 19th centuries, and I had published articles on Lessing and C. F. Meyer—and had recently landed a Twayne Series contract to write on Meyer—I had come to their attention. Adding that Michael Mann was looking forward to helping me "adjust" and all, and Gret and he were eager to get to know Diane (Vreuls), my wife, and me better, Politzer didn't need to sweeten the offer much when we talked salary and benefits.

Though I initially accepted the appointment, which would be subject to ratification by the state—just routine, Politzer had said—the summer dragged on and the California legislature would not meet till mid-September. What if ...? soon reared its head. Meanwhile, to my surprise, John Kurtz, the steady, even-tempered chair at Oberlin, redoubled his efforts to convince me to remain at Oberlin. Coupled with rising fears of how expensive living in Berkeley might be, worrying about uprooting with our two tiny tots now in tow, I wrote Politzer: "With great regret, but huge thanks for your invitation ... I've decided to remain at Oberlin after all." He and Michael Mann sent me a postcard a few days later: "Bedauern wir," which unlike Hesse's "wohl" has many more disparate meanings; i.e. "sympathize"; "regret"; "pity"; "deplore"; "lament." As the years went by, Michael and I exchanged fewer and fewer postcards, trailing off to a Christmas card or two till 1977 showed up on the calendar.

As one doesn't forget where one happened to be when something awful happened (9/11 et al.), I'll not forget helping myself to coffee in Rice Faculty Lounge the morning of January 4—it was winter-term, a lazy month what with most students off on self-designed projects, just a few classes underway—when a colleague, who knew of my friendship with Michael, motioned me over to the couch and whispered, "Have you heard Michael

Mann died yesterday?" My heart began pounding through my chest, and I fell back over an arm of the couch as he leaned over me.

"Just walk me back to my office," I said. After he got me into the stuffed chair in the corner I liked students to relax in during conferences, he said he'd put a note on my door not to disturb. I recall not answering the phone as it rang again and again, just sitting and staring at the wall, till the red numerals on the desk clock blinked 5:00 and I knew I'd have to head home or my family might worry.

The reports varied over the next months, some saying Michael died of a heart attack at home in Orinda (which the *NY Times'* obituary records); others intimating alcohol and drugs were an issue. Randall Jarrell comes to mind: did he actually intend to walk out into traffic, or was he struck by a mindless driver? Oh, Michael, as Peter Bichsel said when Günter Eich died, "even if he died he could have stuck around."

Sorry, I Don't:
Remembering Günter Grass

I

IN the '60s, David Young and I received an Oberlin College grant—to foster faculty development in ancillary interests—that enabled us to visit a number of German poets in hopes of putting together a textbook, which would present a selection of their poems, followed by a series of questions we put to them, and ending with their responses. Some colleagues, knowing full well that we were just beginning to make a mark with our own translations and poems, wondered, as indeed we also did, whether or not the likes of Günter Eich and his mate Ilse Aichinger, Günter Grass, Paul Celan, Karl Krolow, Hilde Domin, Helmut Heißenbüttel, and Rainer Brambach, all on their way to illustrious careers, would open the door for relative unknowns. But open the door they all did, which alas did not result in our ever completing said textbook, but did begin life-long relationships and result in many translations they allowed us to publish through the years.

After productive visits with others, we flew on to Berlin to meet with Grass. Having been advised by a colleague to stay at the Hotel Continental there, we slept the first night rather fitfully, excited at the prospect of attending Brecht's *Threepenny Opera* at the Berliner Ensemble theater in East Berlin the next day, thanks to Helene Weigel. We'd written her hoping to include some of

23

Brecht's poems in the textbook, about which she might answer some questions. Thanks to her invitation on official stationery of the Berliner Ensemble, transiting Checkpoint Charlie to enter the East Zone was a breeze. Alas, when we arrived at the box office, she sent a note down from her quarters that she was indisposed, but trusted we'd enjoy the performance from her personal box. David and I revisit this occasion during our bimonthly lunches, among a host of other shared experiences over the course of a special friendship that's lasted since we were both hired at Oberlin in 1961.

Having written to each writer in advance with an offer to bring anything special they might prize as a gift, we heard from Grass on the usual postcard he communicated with that he'd not mind having some decent if not Cuban cigars — at the time there were embargoes in effect — and his cognac supply was running low. So of course we scoured Berlin for the best cigars and cognac we could buy, which required some justifying when we presented our receipts to Oberlin's comptroller upon return.

Preceding him when he opened the door, that bushy mustache! Steel-rimmed glasses recalled Brecht's. Slightly hunched, if he'd straightened up he'd have topped our heights. A no-nonsense look about him, not one to shake your hand lightly, he then gestured, bowing slightly, toward a staircase after securing our gift package under an arm. Up we trudged, huffing and puffing by the time we reached what might have been the third of fourth floor and were shown into something of a gymnasium, with a basketball hoop at one end and ample space for the gang of kids running about, now busy skirmishing over a soccer ball, now shooting a basketball at the hoop. At the far end, a little spiral staircase led up to a platform overlooking the playing field below. "My eagle's nest," I think he said, and allowed as how he liked writing up there to the background "music" of the neighborhood kids playing with Grass' below.

Let's have one of your cigars before we find out exactly why you're here," he said and, noticing the cognac, "something of a chaser." Opening a drawer in the desk, he parked nifty little shot glasses in a row between us. We took out copies of his poems we wanted to include in the anthology, but before outlining the project, mentioning the other poets who'd be aboard, I took a moment to warm up the atmosphere by way of letting Grass know his work in general was being taught by all of us in Oberlin's German Department; and recounted that only recently, during a discussion of his spell-binding novella *Cat and Mouse* in my conversation class, there was knock at the door. I shouted *"Herein,"* and a man quickly entered, austere looking albeit nattily attired, likely a European judging from his look, his haircut. I pointed to a seat in the back and he waved, then put a finger to his lips, which got the class smiling. It wasn't Parents' Weekend, but on occasion parents would ask to sit in on a class; and we quickly returned to the text at hand. After the class filed out when the bell rang, the man approached me rather stiffly, bowing his head slightly, and, I underlined for Grass, softly clicked his heels together; reminiscent of actors portraying German officials, I couldn't resist adding. To this day I can hear the man enunciating his name crisply — Wernher von Braun — and the few words of thanks he offered in formal German, ending on "quite interesting." Only after he left did it come to me, Iris von Braun, a student in class, must be his daughter! "That calls for another shot of cognac," Grass said, and proposed a toast, "c'est la vie!"

After Grass approved the list of poems we wanted to include, we asked some questions on two accounts: ours, to make sure we basically understood the poems; and slightly less complex ones we hoped would help the students taking them on. Aside from teasing us about applying a double standard, stopping painfully short of suggesting we were dumbing them down, Grass startled us by insisting that all references in the poems could be tracked down; in encyclopedias, library archives, even public records and almanacs.

Our time was up, but before Grass showed us out he suggested — if we were interested and had time (I think we'd have rebooked a flight if we had to!) — we might join him at a rehearsal of his new play, *The Plebeians Rehearse the Uprising*, at the Schiller Theater the following day. We found him hunkered down in one of the back rows of the darkened auditorium and slipped into a row behind. During the hour or so we decided it was polite and prudent to stay, he whispered an occasional remark over his shoulder while scribbling away at a clipboard, but all I recall is a single sentence that has stuck to this day: "No one has the courage to tell me what isn't working!" Whispering our great thanks, we crept out. A few weeks after returning to Oberlin, David recalls our getting a book of Grass' poems he'd inscribed in a tiny script, "Vielen Dank für die europäischen Zigarren!" We dutifully donated the book to the library's Special Collections. David has since opined that Grass hoped the new play would establish him as more than worthy of assuming Brecht's mantle, given Grass' support of striking workers, whereas Brecht had chosen to remain silent during the uprising in East Germany in June, 1953, when threats of Soviet intervention restored "order." At the time, to add insult to the workers' pleas for help from Brecht and others of his station and stature, Brecht was adapting Shakespeare's *Coriolanus* with his Berliner Ensemble compatriots. (The finished version would not be staged till 1962.)

2

In the '90s, when I was working with Karl Krolow on a volume of his selected poems and staying in an inn southeast of Darmstadt, I hiked over to Reichelsheim, where Krolow had recommended I could enjoy a "respectable lunch with decent local wine." After several espressos to stay awake after the repast, I strolled around the picturesque town before heading back to my digs, mindful I'd promised the elderly innkeeper to exercise his chow chow. Just before it was time to hurry back, my eye caught sight of a poster in the city hall's window advertising a public reading, the very next day, by Günter Grass, in the hall's auditorium! Hopeful Krolow would understand my request to postpone our get-together a day—which he was glad to do provided I'd furnish a review—I knew I'd have an early hike back to have a chance at a seat for the noon reading, as I recall the poster read. Dimly aware that Grass had just published a new novel, which a number of critics had found wanting. I'd also heard from a friend in Berlin that Grass was thinking of sticking it to the critics by going on a tour of much smaller venues, defiantly not large cities in which he was accustomed to reading; but, my friend reported, small towns and even villages of his "real readers."

Though I arrived an hour early, it was clear from the throng already lining the hallway to the auditorium and spooling out into the street, waiting for the chamber to open, that I stood a slim chance of getting in at all, much less finding a seat. Nonetheless, I did what others were doing, this not being the U.K. and queuing not even a lost art, and wedged into the crowd. Minutes later someone announced with a megaphone that though the doors would soon open, we were to remain in place as Herr Grass and his entourage would be arriving at any moment to take their seats on the stage. We turned around toward the street and there he was, exiting a limousine. His frame had perhaps filled out some since our encounter some thirty years ago, but nothing else seemed different as he approached, save for graying hair and, more notably, heavily-lidded eyes. Moments after he passed the clump I stood in, he suddenly stopped when the man with the megaphone reached him and whispered something. Now turned toward the chamber whose doors were wide open, we could see a long table on the stage. The next thing I knew Grass himself began tapping a few of us on the shoulder, upon which we were hustled along after him by staff and directed toward the table on the stage. Later we learned Grass was eager to have as many of us seated as possible, no matter where! After Grass took his seat stage center, the man who'd introduce him—perhaps the mayor?—sat down immediately to his right, and next to him, as instructed, me, myself, and I! My brain couldn't stop buzzing. It did occur to me that, while the introduction droned on, Grass had perhaps singled me out because he recognized me somehow from our visit long ago.

Not having come with the new novel for him to sign, nor having read so much as a sentence, I listened half distracted. Like Grass and all of us at the table, I looked out at the audience seated in a bowl the chamber's shape assumed, and my eyes began swimming. I recall Grass reading clearly but softly, like a good actor not melodramatically, which some of the humorous passages might have invited. When he turned the last page of the chapter he read from, pushing back to stretch out, carefully removing his glasses, at first there was a hushed silence before someone began clapping methodically, one clap following another slowly, eventually building to a crescendo the crowd joined in on more and more forcefully till the whole chamber seemed to rumble. Finally, with a light wave, Grass brought the applause to a halt, and someone announced a line could form for those with the novel to sign. For a moment, I thought I might just lean over, say my thanks, reference our visit back when. That quickly became impossible, as the rest of us were hurried off the stage, so I decided to get in line for a word. Once again, queuing was on no one's mind; just scrambling, in groups of three or four, was clearly the rule.

Moving along slowly, I rehearsed a few lines I might risk after adding my thanks for a moving reading, which it had clearly been though I was much adrift: the whole assemblage had reverberated with reverence it would have been hard to escape. The closer I got to Grass, the more nervous I grew, sensing my voice dwindling.

When I was next, I suddenly felt weak and had to brace myself with both palms on the table, trying not to lean too close. He'd been looking down, fumbling with his pen. When he looked up, he seemed to look straight through me to the woman behind. My brain cramp subsided and I blurted out "Niedstraße 14! Where my colleague and I visited you in Berlin, wonder if you remember, sir?" — foolishly hoping that, by mentioning an actual address, he would remember. But then what? He was now looking at the woman next in line as if to say, what's with this guy? My last words tumbled out, "Surely you recall the cigars and cognac we brought you?!" — which to this moment makes me cringe.

His last words were, "Sorry, I don't …" All Krolow did when I recounted the tale the next day was pat me on the hand, which was still trembling.

3

All that was some years before Grass' long-kept "secret" was finally revealed, which he spent many of his remaining years trying to address — saying famously, "It was a weight on me"; not only to rebut his fiercest critics, some of whom, even now that he's gone, remain convinced his intent all along was to "cover up," fudge details, downright dissemble. What we know for sure when he was "outed" is that he had indeed joined the Hitlerjugend (at age 10!), as was almost de rigueur. Barely seventeen, Grass was drafted into the "Waffen-SS," Heinrich Himmler's brainchild, the armed wing of the Nazi Party's SS organization, ultimately condemned at Nuremberg for its criminal acts. At that age, like so many young souls, Grass was easily caught up in the grandeur and pomp, in my view. Some of his detractors claim he did so with excessive fervor and pride, noting he volunteered for submarine duty, a command enjoying great popularity and respect among the populace. However, he was instead assigned to a tank unit and eventually captured in that command. For a moving and I believe faithful account of those years, his essay, "How I Spent the War," which appeared in the June 4th, 2007 issue of *The New Yorker*, is essential reading.

Yellowing notes have recently brought me back to that unnerving day in the '60s when I was teaching Grass' *Cat and Mouse*, as mentioned earlier. Caught up in the thrall of the plot, easily identifying with the young protagonists who dive down to explore a sunken Polish sub, among other adventures, and in which an Iron Cross figures powerfully, my students always got around to wondering how they might have responded, behaved, in those fearful circumstances. However, back then, it never occurred to any of us, as it finally does now, that Grass was making his tortured way through his own submerged ruins, as he surely was throughout all his work. How I'd want him to know Adrienne Rich's "Diving into the Wreck"! Unless of course he did …

Options:
Remembering Calvin Hernton[1]

I

MISSED more and more these days of turmoil and turgidity, Calvin would call you up somehow sensing you were down in the dumps about the world wilding away, and rasp, "Drop everything, don't bother changing your jockstrap. I'll honk in five minutes; we're getting drunk at "The Point," a tavern now long since razed from where it squatted on a corner east of town; and which he did one dreary, stormy night when he drove Bruce Weigl and me to knock back a few brews you couldn't come by in our dry town.

Bruce and I get around to reminiscing about that night, etched in what's left of memory's storehouse, when Calvin, who could hold his liquor better, suddenly yanked us away from the bar, hustling us the hell out of there. Turns out, someone down a few stools had drawn a nasty knife and stabbed someone else. An obituary of sorts, here's some of Calvin's blockbuster ballad that once hung framed over said bar:

---

1   He was said to have been named by his grandmother, who thought highly of President Calvin Coolidge, something of a Civil Rights champion in his day, who among other deeds gave an inspiring Commencement Address at Howard University.

31

THE POINT

It is where you shall be begrudged and beguiled.
It is the place, time and circumstance of your origin,
and it is the source of your most ardent pursuit.
…
It is September 1970, the year of moon and honey.
Get in your red automobile and head one block south
to Lorain Street which is Ohio State Hyway #10.
Turn left and ease on down the road destined in
the direction of The Point.
…
Pause and reflect.
Look straight down Hyway 58.
See the captured runway rescued by the two halves
of the town of Oberlin in process —
Do not continue down that road! Do not follow that
    procession!
Do not go to Wellington!
…
Pause and reflect.

For The Point is more than the leaning men and their
laughter and the drinking …
Here they come, the old, the young, the fisherman with
his homemade reel … the silent one with his bag of
cigarettes … the federal aviation boys with the wreckage
of jet airplanes in their brains, the three friendly pigs
of Oberlin and the one poet in whose breast an agony bleeds
from a secret universality among the dogs of The Point

and by every living beast in the devil damned town …[2]

2

If I'd known of Calvin's history before Oberlin College was fortunate enough to land him or I'd had the good sense to draw him out more, I'd have learned he co-founded *Umbra* (with Langston Hughes, Ishmael Reed, and Alice Walker), one of the most influential literary magazines in its day. That should have led to our inviting him to be a co-editor when colleagues and I founded *Field*. At least I had the good sense, when we were launching the new writing program, to enlist his services to supervise students on their advanced writing projects. Black Studies (so named at the time), his parent department, was generous to allow him to do so.

At that time, late '70s, Calvin published his monumental tome, *The Sexual Mountain and Black Women Writers: Adventures in Sex, Literature, and Real Life*, which earned him many a devoted reader but also a number of serious "enemies." I recall his joking about that with Gary Snyder, whom we'd invited for a reading and lecture,[3] who himself was being followed around by a "Truth Squad" of Native Americans and heckled whenever they perceived Gary had "stolen" a word or phrase from their literature and culture. Calvin had come at the last minute to hear Gary. The only seat open was in the back row, otherwise taken up by the Native Americans.

Sweating some but deftly deflecting some of their loud

---

2 "The Point" appeared in *Pocket Pal* (2/3, Spring 1977), a magazine founded and edited by Bruce Weigl. The three pigs may reference an item in the Lost & Found column in Oberlin's weekly newspaper: "Lost! Nine nice pigs!"

3 The lecture, "Poetry, Community, and Climax," appeared in 1978 in *Field*.

concerns, Gary was ready to cool off when they finally left. After he signed books, we hustled him off to Presti's at the other edge of town from The Point, where we thought we'd enjoy quieter surroundings, less likely to be interrupted by a flashing knife. If only! After many a chaser, sparks began flying, arguments intensified over who knows what, a fist or two landed on other flesh, and glassware flew around till someone called the cops. Haven't checked, but possibly The Police Blotter in the local paper made mention of "the brawl."

3

As the years went by, Calvin made valuable suggestions and other contributions to the writing program's curriculum, among them a willingness to engage with playwriting students as well as poets and fiction writers. The rest of us, occasionally teaching playwriting, hadn't, as Calvin had, actually written plays. Word eventually got around that Calvin had even had his plays staged in many a venue. Once students got past his rugged appearance, set off by the darkest shades money could buy, heard the humor in his occasional scowl, and sensed the reservoir of tenderness below, more and more of them signed up happily to work with him. Passing around his fierce novel, *Scarecrow*, and *Medicine Man*, his book of dramatic narrative poems as well, they basked in his fostering ways. I dreamt the College would let him transition to becoming a permanent member of the writing program. Alas, Calvin was comfortable in his own department, hence he was reluctant to work with writing students exclusively, because his interests, personal and pedagogical, took him into a wide range of fields, e.g. philosophy, politics, psychology, and sociology.[4] So we went about deepening our working and personal relationship in other ways. Two instances should suffice to underline how much I'll forever be in debt to him.

4

The spring Odetta appeared in concert at Finney Chapel, Calvin, as he was wont to do, called up out of the blue. "Know you and Diane wouldn't miss Odetta, so how'd you two like to hang out some with her and a few friends afterward at my house after she sends the crowd home happier than they've been for a while?" He could likely hear my heart skip. What he didn't know, however, was that Odetta had her own surprise in store for him, whose birthday she knew was close enough to concelebrate. Who should be in Calvin's tiny kitchen, stirring away at a monster pot of jambalaya, a bright bandana swathing her forehead, but Maya Angelou, who had flown in and slipped into Calvin's always open house unseen. If only we'd had a camera to immortalize his gaping smile! It was one of the few times I ever saw him remove his shades, to wipe a tear away.

After we'd recovered some from the sumptuous feast and exchanged a dozen toasts, we sprawled at Odetta's and Maya's feet. The two had settled on the sofa and began humming back and forth till their hums morphed into bits and pieces, finally into full-blown many-versed songs we later learned they'd known from childhood, none of which had been recorded. The afterglow

---

4 Other books by Calvin Hernton: *White Papers for Americans; Sex and Racism in America; Coming Together: Black Power, White Hatred, and Sexual Hang-ups; Cannabis Experience: An interpretative Study of the Effects of Marijuana and Hashish; The Red Crab Gang and Black River Poems*

lasted all summer long.

5

For unknown reasons, Calvin and I drifted apart for a while until he up and called early one morning. "Can you ride shotgun on my stage? Gotta get to Cleveland to fetch two gals, one of whom's gigging here this weekend. Grunt if you can be on the curb in five minutes." I managed a grunt, he hung up, and I plunged into some clothes to make curbside just as he pulled up.

It was clear he wasn't going to tell me who our passengers back to town would be, so we settled for some chat about the literary scene, avoiding campus politics, which we both loathed. Looking back now, I wish I'd interviewed him more about his past. The few times I did try to open that window, he shut it abruptly; so we let the radio crackle away the last few miles to the hotel where our mysterious passengers awaited us.

Never having seen pictures of them, I just saw warm visages, their exaggerated waves directed solely at Calvin, who'd bounded out of the car and was swept up in hearty hugs. Once the threesome separated, "Hi, I'm Audre, who are you?" floated my way. Before I could reply, the other woman said, equally sweetly, "Hi, I'm Toni," as I grabbed her suitcase before she could, while Calvin met me at the trunk with Audre's.

All I recall from the charged, exciting exchanges among them was what Audre said in a lull: "OK folks, what's your favorite poem?" As with one voice, they all broke out chanting, "Sundays too my father got up early / and put his clothes on in the blueblack cold" … Too embarrassed to ask whose poem it was, I vowed to myself I'd track it down and memorize it, and

I've recited it daily ever since.[5]

6

Though Calvin never shirked Black Studies commitments, he continued to find ways to work with our writing students. The last few years, before retiring, I was able to persuade him to join us in personnel decisions, which he undertook extremely seriously, often counseling the whole staff in difficult situations.

When Bruce Weigl returned to town to teach at Lorain County Community College, he and Calvin became even faster friends. They remained so until Calvin died some weeks after 9/11. Bruce had readily agreed to Calvin's wish that he serve as executor of Calvin's estate. Having been told that along with Calvin's wife Bruce spent Calvin's last hours with him, I asked Bruce if he could share something of what those hours were like. Here's what Bruce has allowed me to quote: "Mary and I were sitting on the bed. It was late, one or two in the morning; and we'd been waiting for a late-night delivery service to rush some meds to help Calvin get through things. He was mostly quiet, his breathing labored. Suddenly, he sat straight up and, without opening his eyes, very clearly said 'options,' then fell back and stopped breathing. My instinct was to try to resuscitate him, but Mary reminded me it was time to let him go, so I didn't. After Calvin said 'options,' I looked at Mary with surprise, even asked her what that could mean. She could only shake her head.

"While I had no idea what Calvin meant, over the years I've thought about it; and now believe I have some sense of what he meant. At the moment of passing, something important must

---

5   "Those Winter Sundays" is Robert Hayden's perfect poem. I'm forever grateful to Audre Lorde, Toni Morrison, and Calvin Hernton for having taught it to me.

have occurred to him about how we live, then stop living, and
what it all means. That was also the subject of his best work. It felt
good and warm knowing it wasn't the end of Calvin, but another
kind of beginning, how he saw it on his way out."[6]

6   From an e-mail from Bruce Weigl.

White Asparagus:
Remembering Tankred Dorst

I

GIFTING me with one of his books I most cherish, *Wie Im Leben Wie Im Traum* (Suhrkamp Verlag. 1990/As in Life As in Dream), he inscribed it in something of a fragile hand: "Dear Stuart, I recall my time in Oberlin so fondly! When will we see each other again? I'm greeting, embracing you. Your old Tankred. Oct. 9, 2014." He managed to live three more years, but I never got to hug him again.

In 1970, we of the German Department at Oberlin were astonishingly unanimous about inviting Tankred to be the third Max Kade German Writer-in-Residence.[1] Peter Spycher and I'd begun teaching a bit of his work, especially the scary, wickedly mordant farce, *Die Kurve* (The Curve), which engendered so much enthusiasm among students it convinced us to propose Tankred's name. All I recall from the drive back from the airport, interrupted for some food and brews, was Tankred admonishing us not to get so "tanked" that Peter and I would miss a "curve" on the way back to Oberlin.

Besides teaching a seminar on his own work, Tankred was

---

1   For a biographical overview of Tankred Dorst's life and letters, as well as a note from him about his stay at Oberlin, see *Willkommen und Abschied*: Thirty-five Years of German Writers-in-Residence at Oberlin College (Edited by Dorothea Kaufman and Heidi Thomann Tewarson/Camden House 2005).

39

ever generous about visiting others' classes, as well as attending rehearsals of his play, *Die Mohrin*, which I'd decided to direct in my German studio theater course. He even wielded a hammer helping us build the set, notably a fanciful little boat he himself designed, which lived on as my kids' adventure-craft, prominently moored in our backyard till the elements laid it waste. For some time, Tankred and I exchanged postcards: T: "Is it still 'afloat'?" S: "Yep. Still shipshape."

Thanks to Ellen Johnson, Oberlin's preeminent art historian, who identified and championed emerging artists early on who would become more and more prominent, souls like Dine, Oldenburg, and Rauschenberg were invited to campus for extensive residencies. Learning of their presence, devotion, and gifts to Oberlin,[2] Tankred was doubly delighted because he had followed and admired their work. Was it Tankred's or my idea to project the image of Rauschenberg's "Bed" on a wall, in which the play's lovers, Aucassin and Nicolette, spend a night in a seedy hotel while fleeing their pursuers? In any event, Tankred and I shared a passion for stage business; and spent perhaps more time doodling notions back and forth for how to keep the "images" flowing than attending to the rehearsals' problems.[3]

After Tankred returned to what he called "Little Europe," having given a series of readings and talks at American universities once his Kade time was over at Oberlin, a group

---

2 Oldenburg's "Giant Three-Way Plug" was installed in 1970 during Dorst's residency, and I wish I had a picture of Tankred climbing all over it when he learned it wasn't "forbidden"!

3 Tankred especially loved hearing of Hume Croyn's "business" in *The Miser*, at the Guthrie Theater in Minneapolis in 1963: when The Miser sneezed, he skirted around the stage chasing bits of snuff his nose had ejected. I loved hearing of Tankred's idea of having Friedrich Engels' father, who owned a textile factory in England in which young Engels worked for a time, yank great bolts of cloth off the walls in a cavernous hall and slowly wind them around his son till he mummified him. Alas, so far as I know, Tankred never finished the play I believe he intended to call *Engels*.

of students painted the "rock," a large boulder in the square, as they'd sometimes do to praise or mourn a soul or an event: "Tankred is gone," is all it said or had to say. He wrote to say he was going to be sure to preserve the Polaroid we sent him of said rock.[4]

2

Some time later Tankred sent me the script of his film, *Sand*, which premiered on German TV in 1971. Directed by the noted Peter Palitzsch, it centers on the political assassin Karl Ludwig Sand, who stabbed to death August Friedrich Ferdinand von Kotzebue, a highly popular German dramatist who detested liberals and opposed free institutions. Sand, a theology student, was a militant member of the *Burschenschaften*, and Kotzebue's murder gave Metternich the pretext to issue the *Carlsbad Decrees*, effectively disbanding the *Burschenschaften*, as well as targeting the liberal press and egregiously restricting academic freedom in the states of the German Confederation. In short, the "subject" was ideally made for Dorst's theatrical politics, aesthetics and primal impulses, front and center in his strongest work.

As soon as I read *Sand*, I wrote Tankred for permission to make a film of it with our students, with Peter Bichsel in a supporting role, who was at the time (1972) yet another Kade visiting writer. Peter was an admirer of Dorst's work in general and his powerful drama *Toller* in particular, hence equally enthusiastic about the

---

4   "The End of Playwriting," the talk he wrote in Oberlin to deliver on his tour, went over wonderfully when he tried it out on us before leaving on his final tour. As he's written, he played with the notion that future theater could do without playwrights. Perhaps someone knows where there might be a print copy?!

prospect.[5]

Peter joined me to scout the landscape for possible scene locations. Oberlin's in the middle of fertile farmland, with many a side and back road we coursed to key on two primary "sets": an old, out of the way wall of some sort, would serve a crucial scene; some sort of old schoolhouse as a setting for important deliberations. My old Taunus, a Ford import from its German counterpart that never took hold, was on its last legs, but I assured Peter if it gave out a farmer would likely tractor-tow us back to town, as had in fact happened previously. Both Tankred and Peter had fun with its name, though having been a student in Germany, I actually knew more of the Taunus mountain range's fauna and flora for having hiked there, and teased them back in spades.

Just west of town, we sighted what I remembered was a collapsing structure—many an older Oberlin building is of soft brick from a nearby quarry—that was in use as a corncrib and might offer up an ideal wall to stage the crucial scene. I was telling Peter the police blotter in the local rag occasionally reported kids playing there, who had to be chased away for fear one might suffocate under a sudden shift in the cob-mass, when a dog shot out of nowhere, barking so fiercely we thought it might hurtle through an open window. I swerved and must have caught it under a tire. By its shriek we suspected it was dead. Sure enough, and just as we parked to see about its slumped shape, a farmer wielding a pitchfork came running across the field shouting what turned out, to our relief, to be curses at his "damn dog." He even apologized, as the "critter" had caused other cars to swerve

---

5   Both Tankred and Peter were amused to learn I'd once tried to entice Peter Lorre to play the lead in Brecht's early one-act, *Die Eisenhandlung*, joined by our student actors. Alas, Lorre died in the midst of negotiations to bring him to campus.

dangerously! After adding our regrets for the dog's demise, sensing the corncrib might belong to him, I asked his permission to explore it for the film. He grinned when I asked him to spell his name so I could thank him in the credits if the film came off.

After we tumbled around on the mountains of stored corn inside, lobbing cobs in each other's direction like kids on the first day of summer vacation, Peter hooting to my hollering, I surprised, not to say scared him a bit after we dusted off, by brandishing two knives I'd been concealing. "Sand had armed himself with two knives in case one wouldn't suffice," I said, "when he tracked Kotzebue to his new abode in Mannheim, soon after he'd settled his family there." Peter ran his finger down the blade of the one I gave him and drew blood, which he promptly licked up. An actor himself to the core, he dangled his hand as if severely wounded, but recovered nicely to join me stabbing in myriad ways at the crumbling brick wall. I wanted to be sure it would hold up when David Walker, playing Sand, practiced murdering Kotzebue in rehearsals. Incidentally, the wall suffered David going at it over and over again quite well, first with one knife, then the other.[6]

---

6 I'd already cast most roles, especially Sand's and his most trusted friend's. Imagine having not only David Walker in your class, one of our most gifted, downright brilliant students ever, who's since become one of Oberlin's most beloved professors—and incidentally also teaches at times in the Writing Program, co-edits *Field*/OC Press as well—but also Franz Wright (R.I.P.)—who with James Wright, his father, are the only father-son poets to win the Pulitzer Prize—whom I cast as Sand's best friend. John Mahnke—R.I.P.—perhaps the most promising poet-in-spe of the lot—played another member of Sand's inner circle. While Bruce Weigl, another of the amazing young poets taking the class and currently one of America's most prominent authors, didn't try out for a part, he offered valuable suggestions all along.

3

Because Peter had to go off for a spell giving readings elsewhere, I took Paul Buck along to scout for an additional structure, as the corn crib proved too cramped for our actions. A student in German as well as an art major, Paul was also a skilled photographer, and readily agreed to film the script with equipment on loan from the Art Department. Several days into circling the surrounding landscape, often stopping to boot up to explore under- and backwoods, we finally came across an old red brick schoolhouse collapsing in on itself, sitting back a hundred yards or so from the road. Paul lugged his tripod and cameras along to take a number of shots we could use to draft the scene's action — the *Burschenschaften* gang Sand had managed to conscript to plot a course of action that would result in catching Kotzebue at an unguarded moment to dispatch.

With a decent storyboard to work from, rehearsing away in a classroom at the college, we finally caravanned out on a weekend, prepared to camp overnight at the site to build "believability" into the scene, exposing bodies and temperaments to the night's effects. So-called best laid plans were alarmingly interrupted not long after we set up camp among the ruins and reconnoitered to identify hazards — rusty nails sticking out; glass shards hidden by grass; jagged wood sticking out of dark places: a familiar siren pierced our ears, and soon after, breaking through the underbrush, a nattily clad State Trooper strode toward me, likely taking me to be in charge of our motley group. The farmer who owned the land must have spotted Paul and me earlier, so when we returned he called the cops.

The trooper came straight to the point: "You are trespassing, sir!" Perhaps he said it more politely than I heard it, but, rattled, I made the mistake of sputtering something in German, which we'd been speaking among ourselves to keep the script alive. "Excuse me?" he said more pointedly, and took a step closer, at which the students clotted together, looking worried as well. Recovering my senses, I blurted out, "Oops, guess we should have asked someone's permission to be out here ..." "You've got that right, sir." Babbling on about why we were there, I must have satisfied the trooper enough because he began to smile when it was apparent we were up to a harmless pursuit. "The owner would appreciate your heading over to his house a.s.a.p.," he softened his voice. Directing our attention to a house we could barely make out through the foliage, he saluted smartly, touched the brim of his hat, even advised us to be careful "what with the debris out here," and left. Days later, the gang was still exchanging snappy salutes among themselves. As with the owner of the corncrib, the fellow who owned the film site was happy to have his name listed in the credits. When Peter and Tankred got the full report I filed with them, as well as with the chairman of the German Department to cover my "professional" tracks, they went on teasing me mercilessly again. After showing the film to German classes, I had a copy made for Tankred and Peter, but have since looked in vain for the original in the German Department's nooks and crannies: LOST, still ...

4

When I wrote Tankred I'd be passing through Munich while touring my last book of German poems, he offered me a bed for a few days if I had time to "visit and renew our friendship."[7] White asparagus, he'd written, would be right in season so be prepared to eat them around the clock, he joked, or so I thought

---

7   *Nicht Hinauslehnen* had just been published by Delp Verlag (1975), in Bad Windsheim, close by Munich where Dorst and his mate, Ursula Ehler, had settled down.

at first! However, there they were on lunch and dinner plates for several days, albeit dressed up variously, and always prepared to perfection by both Tankred and Ursula (Ehler), by then his wife, and since the 1970s his co-collaborator in spades, hearts, clubs, and diamonds. Indeed, I know of no other writer, major or minor, who has left us so many works—some thirty plays, at least eight story collections and novels, four major films, and several translations—co-written with anyone, not to mention with a mate. It was clear from being around them even for a bit that their hearts fairly seemed to beat as one, hang the clichéd sentiments of many a sappy song; and if I'd not lost the journal I kept on that trip, I could cite exchanges between them as if spoken by one mind, which I couldn't help but record for their apercus and wit.

Having to post a letter the day I left—Ursula and Tankred were driving me to the airport—what I still recall vividly is what happened while we were waiting in line at the P.O.'s window. By way of already beginning to say goodbye, I finally shared one of my family's fondest memories, of Tankred's coming to our house in Oberlin for supper. I reminded him that as soon as we'd introduced him to our kids, then five and seven, he tenderly lifted them up by the hands to the top of his shoes and began skating them about, which we then kept doing in his memory till they got too big for us.

While I babbled on, I could see Ursula's and Tankred's gaze drifting. I'd been somewhat aware a couple in line ahead of us were having something of a heated argument, but it turns out Ursula and Tankred were recording virtually every word the couple exchanged. Waiting till we were back in the car, they let loose, reenacting the scene out to the syllable! Tankred: "Did you hear her say to him …!; Ursula: "And did you hear her rejoinder …!" They laughed their sweet together-laugh when I said, "OK Dearies. I'll look for the whole back and forth in your next play!"

Now that Tankred's gone and died — when Günter Eich died, Peter Bichsel lamented, "He could have gone ahead and died if he'd only stuck around longer." I pray that Ursula, wherever she is now, is in a good patch, and for sure she must know what bountiful, great gifts they've left to the rest of us.

Friends, Let's Tell the Truth:[1] Remembering Rossi, Rizzardi, & Raboni

I

SOME thirty-five years ago, the guest-presenter in my translation workshop, a dear friend and colleague, Vinio Rossi, introduced us to the poetry of Giovanni Raboni. Vinio began with brief remarks about major issues of translating from Italian, and he discussed Raboni's work against the background of Italian literature. He handed out "the literals," a five-part sequence including "The Washerwoman," "Surgeon," "The Fortune Teller," "The Baker," and:

THE CARPENTER

If you seek
you find. If you want to save some wood,
instead of nailing it into a square
or an isosceles triangle or a circle,
you can make it into a cross.

When Vinio was alive, during one of our "cocktail hours" at Presti's bar, we'd always get back to the immediate aftermath:

---

1 Taken from a Raboni poem.

when Vinio finished walking us through the literals, a student in the front row crossed herself dramatically, then burst into tears and asked to be excused. Only later did we learn she'd been having a crisis of faith, and thanked us after our co-translations were published for connecting her with "a deeply Catholic poet."[2]

Vinio was instrumental in helping us launch Charles Wright's Montale translations in the Field Translation Series. He knew of Raboni's debt of gratitude to Montale, his several books of poems that were making an indelible mark, and his stellar career as a translator as well. So over another glass of Presti's best Chianti, knowing I'd been collaborating on Holub, Vaiciunaite, and Sorescu translations, Vinio proposed writing to Raboni: inasmuch as very few of his poems exist in English, perhaps he'd be interested in our trying to collect enough for a Selected. Not only did Giovanni write right back, he said he'd be delighted to set aside some time if we wanted to get to Milan so we could say, he joked, "the translations have been approved by the author!" As it has in other blessed instances, Oberlin College generously provided a travel grant, Vinio booked us on Alitalia, and next thing we woke up in Rome, eventually making our way to Giovanni's door in Milan after a quick trip to Bologna. Vinio had been corresponding with Rizzardi, a professor and something of a dean at the university there, whose work he'd been following and translating ever since he came across some early Rizzardi poems, in English! They'd appeared in *Poetry*, which we found intriguing.

What a way to get over jet-lag: bask in the delightful, generous, otherworldly company of "Alfredo": after wining and dining us sumptuously in Bologna, he zipped us in his little roadster up to Urbino, where he also taught, having arranged

---

2 *The Coldest Year of Grace: Selected Poems of Giovanni Raboni* (Wesleyan University Press. 1985)

for us to give a talk on how we co-translated to a gathering of literature students. En route, he stopped for gas. "ALFREDO!" shrieked the woman working the pumps when she recognized him, threw her arms around his neck, and whispered what sure seemed like sweet words, first in one ear, then the other. "Why don't you also call me 'Alfredo' from now on," he grinned at us.

Thanks to Vinio's virtually native Italian, we somehow bumbled our way through the talk we'd not taken sufficient pains to organize. While attending to university business, Alfredo had turned us over to his chief assistant, a graduate student of sorts at the time. It's no surprise, as I Google Gabriella Morisco now, to see what an impressive scholar she's become, with special expertise in American and English literature. She dazzled us with her range of reference, incisive comments on things literary.

As if to make up for not having attended our talk, Alfredo invited us for a nightcap at his lodge on one of Urbino's hills. Aware of *Field* Magazine's use of postcards for covers, after quite a few brandies he pulled something of a shoebox down from a shelf in the library and wondered if we'd like to use one for a future magazine cover. As if reading a card catalogue, we flipped through the astonishing collection: mostly cards actually penned by writers, among them the card we eventually chose for a possible *Field*: James Joyce's handwritten card sent from the Zurich Zoo to his grandson Stephen, then five years old, living in Paris. "I'll only charge you $200 for a one-time use, but you'll need to insure it for $1000 when you send it back," Alfredo said, topping our snifters off with a decent local cognac. We'd not have gasped if we'd known the Joyce-card *Field* issue would sell out, surely thanks to the card's provenance — *Field* covers had already become something of a collector's item! — and especially for his charming, invented tale about what the three monkeys in the image are up to, sitting at a table and slurping soup.[3]

Inserting the card into a padded envelope, Alfredo handed it to Vinio with some remarks in Italian I missed out on, which Vinio couldn't later recall for a few too many passes at the cognac bottle, he pled. Though not a *Field* editor, hence with no authority, Vinio, typically generous beyond the call of duty, urged Alfredo to send some poems to *Field* so they could perhaps appear in the same issue bedecked by the JJ card. I quickly added of course we'd be happy to "consider" any he'd like to try us out on … Generously driving us to catch an early train to Milan the next day, Alfredo said to be sure to greet Raboni for him.

2

We called Raboni from the Hotel Milano Scala, where he'd booked us a room for only $99 a night, though the price list on the door said $239. We figured he had connections, which he didn't deny, as he wouldn't for future breaks we enjoyed during our stay. "Let's use first names," he said, before advising us to keep the large windows in our room open as much as possible to hear any strains from an opera at the Scala close by, which especially

---

3   Translated by Vinio Rossi from the Italian, here's what Joyce wrote to his grandson:

6 April 1937

Caro nipotino: These are the 3 monskeyteers of Zurich. Their names are Athos, Porthos and Aramis. Porthos is in the middle and he makes the most noise with his soup. Athos is on the right and he can out away 2 spoonfuls to the others' one. But Aramis on the left says soup is for saps and what he wants his un singeno di coco.

Such are monskeyteers/NONNO

Back at Oberlin, when Vinio and I met with Oberlin's comptroller, we were at some pains to justify the $200 expense for the card. Listening patiently as we agonized, the princely Arthur Cotton finally shooed us out the door. "Let's don't ever do that again, boys," he pretended to scowl.

gladdened Vinio, a huge opera fan. The shank of the evening still ahead, Giovanni suggested we meet in the cozy, beautifully appointed cocktail lounge at the hotel in an hour, where he said we wouldn't mistake him for one of the opera singers who hang out there. "I'll be an older guy, quite slight, with a scruffy mustache and beard my friends say makes me look even more wigged than usual. But you won't be able to yank them off," he laughed, alluding to the Carole Lombard and Jack Benny film, "To Be or Not To Be," a favorite film, something else we shared!

Showering, while I stretched my aching back on a cushy bed, Vinio provided the only strains I'd hear during our stay; and I joined him in a last "O Sole Mio" flourish, my baritone fading into his sharp tenor. Sinking back into the plush leather couch in the lounge, we were waiting for our aperitif when suddenly the double doors burst open, and in strode a large figure dangling something of a large white handkerchief from his hand, followed by a wedge of an entourage, marching to his tune; and he headed to another, obviously more private, lounge in the back, set off by heavier doors. "Guess who just walked inches by us," Vinio said, and didn't wait for an answer because it was clear I didn't know. "The great Pavarotti, that's who! In my younger years, I'd have schemed to get his autograph." Vinio reminded me we'd seen Pavarotti's picture on a poster tacked to a kiosk. If I'd kept better notes, I'd mention the opera.

Spotting us before we caught sight of him, Giovanni waved the small wave one does to children, and smiled with twinkling eyes when he eased into a leather armchair across from us. We began with a toast to "a possible collection of his selected poems." Tenting his hands, he promised to vet all translations, now and by mail once we returned; and to help clear rights, for affordable fees, he hoped. No email back then, so we understood the project would take considerable time, especially given our day jobs, his as an editor for Mondadori Publishers, still one of Italy's premier houses. He was also devoting himself to a number of his own alliances with foreign poets whose work he wanted to ferry into Italian. We gave him a copy of questions we had about the versions we'd brought for review, which he took time to pore over before raising his glass a last time and folding the sheet crisply, tucking it into his jacket pocket as if it were a handkerchief. Clinking glasses one last time, he proposed we take a day or two just to be in one another's company, get a "feel for each other's predispositions, how we shared the same air" (almost an exact phrase from one of his poems, Vinio and I realized and shared a nod); "and I trust you've got sturdy walking shoes," he added. "I'd like to tour you around the landscape of some of my poems," he said softly, without a trace of self-importance.

We should have trained to be Giovanni's walking companions, who, taking tinier steps, soon left us gasping a yard behind. Our tongues went out at every espresso bar we passed, but mindful of having asked for precious time of one so engaged in the literary life of Milan, not to mention Italy and other lands as well, we didn't beg for mercy, just doubled down on espressos when Giovanni finally said it was time to drink something. He led us to a *ristorante*, run by a friend, who simply tore the bill up when we went to pay.

We'd written in our introduction to the *The Coldest Year of Grace* that Giovanni's poems "seem at times spoken by a prosecuting attorney building a case against waste and corruption in secular and religious circles," and as he led us through "the ruins," given his manner of commenting, he seemed a sort of modern-day Virgil, with "an eye for searing detail and an admonishing tone" you wouldn't want to face as the defendant he was prosecuting before a jury. When Giovanni saw I had something of a sketchbook going—I'd laid it on the bar's table— and learned I especially wanted to bring back images of churches for my wife, he suggested I might want to do a quick "portrait"—a favorite word, we'd already come to know — of the abandoned square bordered by the church of San Lorenzo and a porno movie house, before we moseyed on to the Naviglio, a large basin fed by a canal he'd fished in as a lad. "No one of right mind would eat anything caught there now, of course," he grinned. "It's a Lethe no one ever gets to the other side of."

What began to strike us was the concordance between the voice of his poems and Giovanni's natural way of speaking. Both voices also shared a similar sharpness of silence, a way of breaking off into fragment and allusion, half turning away from both subject and object, to focus, as we'd written, not only on what is essential but equally what must be ignored, or suffer oblivion by drowning in the inconsequential. Catching us flagging with a sudden glance back at us, Giovanni broke off the tour: "Let's take tomorrow as well to enjoy each other's relaxed company before we hover over the poems in my cramped study. Some friends are helping restore *The Last Supper* and will let us watch a bit, if you don't mind sitting on some splintery planks and getting a fine coating of dust, not to mention some in our lungs!"

Ecstatic at the prospect, we assured him our behinds had trained aplenty sitting on bleachers at sporting events. We promised to return the favor if he'd do us the honor of appearing at Oberlin at some point. "Something else to drink to," he said when steering us back to the hotel, joining in a salute to Pavarotti on his kiosk.

All my bones and muscles still recall the grooves and bumps and, yes, splinters, in the plank as we watched the crew restoring *The Last Supper*. I imagine sitting for some three hours as in an upside-down operating theater, watching three souls poised high above on ladders, a woman and two men, in white lab coats, who'd daily, excruciatingly painfully, clean an area the size of a postage stamp with delicate instruments carefully laid out on a tray on the ladder's side-extension, attended by others in gray lab coats below ready to assist with any request. At one point, I had the temerity to nibble on a dry roll I'd stashed in my pocket to head off an occasional siege of hypoglycemia, only to have the whole theater "shut down" and everyone look my way. Giovanni politely helped me brush some crumbs off the plank into my handkerchief, morse-coding me with pats on my knee: n-e-v-e-r-d-o-t-h-a-t-a-g-a-i-n-p-l-e-a-s-e. On the way out, he whispered that any such sound as I'd made could easily be taken for something fluttering down from Leonardo's brushstrokes.

Our nerves a bit frayed, Giovanni asked if we'd mind taking a short cut back to the hotel through the "cemetery of drawers" where his parents were buried, whom he'd not visited in some time. Looking up at a stack of drawers, Giovanni pointed to two, their plaques dull in the slanting sun's rays, his parents' names clearly in need of polishing. Something he liked doing himself, he sighed, but lately he'd been so tied up in projects he'd perhaps have to tip a groundskeeper to ladder up and give them a shine. To give Giovanni a moment alone, Vinio motioned me back a ways. We turned up our collars against the dusk's chill while watching Giovanni slightly sway back and forth as if in a reverie. Noticeably slowing down for the last stretch back to the hotel, he split off when it was clear we could find our way back alone. "Get a good night's sleep for what you're in for tomorrow," he said matter-of-factly.

3

Well aware of Raboni's reputation as a translator himself — his Baudelaire and his Proust versions were widely celebrated — as well as his renown as an essayist on contemporary poetry and poetics: among others, his essays on Auden, Pound, and Eliot were considered required reading — we knocked on his door the next morning with some trepidation. Having graduated to a warm hug, we were led into his study, a mini-museum of paintings and sculpture. His elegant desk, piled high with journals and books, looked out on a small park with bountiful trees. A quiet place to read and think, what an ideal, interior space to find your way to soft-spoken poems on the surface, yet bristling with implications, ideas, and passions. "Speak from a distance or just be quiet," from La Fontaine's *Fables*, Raboni took as an epigraph for one of his books.

What he emphasized again and again was to locate the voices of the poems, making sure, he pled, that they don't sound "translated or stiff: I want the poems to live in your American-English. Make sure they read naturally, spoken by an actual human being!" So much of the rest of our time together consisted of his reading us the originals to fine-tune Vinio's hearing them deeply, as he was my conduit into the sounds of their music. Many of the poems have at least two narrators and multiple "I's," he stressed, while emanating from the poet's head, must ultimately be the reader's to possess; or, as one poem has it, "… the things said and not said / between you, and the person you are / are probably too few or too many …" In the days left, as we smoothed the voices first and foremost, Giovanni also cleared up a few passages where we'd gotten lost following the meaning; and kept reassuring us we were tracking the poems like well-trained bloodhounds. Imagine our relief at hearing from an author we weren't messing up!

The day before departing, we relaxed over a final toast to "us three monskeyteers." (We'd shared the Joyce postcard with him.) All the questions we'd come with, as well as others that came up while working together, Giovanni answered more deeply than we'd bargained for, which led to future headaches! But we'd apparently gained his trust: and knew he was now committed to making sure we'd eventually have a viable manuscript to circulate, so worries something might go amiss gradually ebbed. He sent us back to the hotel with a final surprise: "I've arranged a small dinner later tonight, invited a few friends I'd like you to meet, so I'll pick you up around eight. No need to rent a tuxedo, or even polish your shoes: just come as you are!"

If Vinio were alive, he'd surely recall the name of the restaurant Giovanni seemed to have reserved for our final "banquet," as the dozen of us gathered to wine and dine, then wined some more past midnight without any other patrons in sight. Though Giovanni introduced us at some length to his other guests, whose own accomplishments he enumerated as if presenting them with awards, all I vividly recall is they were prominent writers, artists, and editors. Having had way more to eat and drink than usual, all that's left now is a blurred image of the evening's parameters. If only a tape had been made of final remarks and salutations, especially Giovanni's, concluding with Vinio's *Grazie* in return, delivered in his purest Italian! Knowing he'd likely be asked to say something by way of goodbye as well, Vinio had gone to our hotel's lounge to write out some words. If he had stuck to that script, like a good politician advised to "stay on message," I'd not have much more to add. However, to this day I'm told people still reference Vinio's slip of tongue, which brought the house down! Everyone laughed so loud and so long tears came streaming forth as well, so that I couldn't help but join in, with absolutely no clue of what Vinio had said to prompt the torrent.

No one said anything else of any moment, just kept exchanging looks and laughs till they died out as well. Driving us back to our hotel, Giovanni kept telling Vinio something, patting him on the arm, as if to say "Don't beat yourself up"; while Vinio's expression, frozen from the moment the laughs began, remained distraught. I knew enough to wait till he might be willing to recount exactly what he'd said, about an hour into our flight back.

"Okay, keep your seatbelt buckled," Vinio began. "Remember the dessert? Well, a friend of Giovanni's had specially brought some figs from his grandfather's farm for the centerpiece, about the choicest figs you'd ever eat, not to mention what the pastry chef would do with them." I did sort of recall I'd never quite had anything like them. "Well, in the middle of my little thank-you speech, I thought it might be amusing to end on a note of what a beautiful dinner we'd been treated to, especially with such a finishing flourish, the '*figa*' concoction ... Sober, I damn well know the Italian for 'fig' and it sure ain't '*figa*'!" Let's leave it at that. Your Italian might find it useful for other contexts when you get around to adding it to your vocabulary."

Sorry, But:
Remembering Hilde Domin

I

Midway through our trek in the '60s to interview a number of German poets for an anthology David Young and I hoped to publish as a textbook, we got off the train in Heidelberg. Disappointed we weren't able to arrange visits with more than one woman, we were doubly eager to knock on Hilde Domin's door. We crossed the Neckar to the north part of town, then huffed and puffed our way up the "Philosopher's Way" to find her modest house, its clean Bauhaus lines a relief from traditional architecture.

Surprising us with a firm, double-handed handshake, Hilde exuded a force field of energy to wobble you. Her cheerful, lilting voice kept you from thinking about anything except what might next issue from her lips. She swept us into her studio, where she'd already set out a pot of tea and some ginger-cake I'd read she loved making. "Let's first replenish you," she said, cutting us a slab of cake, "then have ourselves a good walk farther up Heidelberg's famous — or some would say infamous — Philosophenweg, which I can see by your faces has already challenged you. I need to take a brisk walk daily to clear my muddled mind," she added. "Besides, you want to be able to say, as any tourist would, that you took in the splendid view across the river at our castle in the center of the old town. By the way, it's the best-selling postcard,"

61

she grinned impishly.

Before we set off, she demonstrated how gowned philosophers from the university still stride along, arms curved, hands joined as if handcuffed to their backs. On cue, we pinned our arms back and waltzed off singing, "We're off to see the wizard." Hilde allowed as how she'd wanted red shoes ever since seeing Dorothy's. When I mentioned they were on display at the Smithsonian, she said that was yet another reason to visit the States.

Relieved to find a bench when we'd just about run out of breath, we plopped down as she laughed. I dusted the place between David and me, Hilde curtsied, edged in between us, and we sat there in solitude for a while. We'd done research on all the poets who'd agreed to receive us, but her past was hardest to access. Born Hilde Löwenstein, she'd gone off to Italy, we knew, with Erwin Palm, whom she'd met when they were students at the University of Heidelberg. Erwin was on his way to becoming a prominent Latin American scholar, historian, and writer. Hilde, who'd earned a PhD in economics in Florence before the couple married in 1936 and settled in Rome, was also on her way somewhere if more slowly.[1] What we didn't know was why she'd begun publishing as Hilde Domin, so we risked asking her.

Clearly pained, she was reluctant to offer much more than a summary of what were surely momentous, even traumatic times they'd had to endure. The rise of Mussolini, the pall of Fascism over the city choking them, they began frantic efforts to emigrate. After making it to England in 1939, they set their sights across the Atlantic. No surprise in retrospect given what we know of the hideous, immoral politics at the time, their entry-applications to the U.S., Mexico, Argentina, and Brazil were rejected except in

----

1 Erwin Walter Palm (1910-1988): see Wikipedia for details of his illustrious achievements and awards. Hilde Löwenstein Palm Domin (1909-2006): see Wikipedia for her considerable achievements and awards as well.

a few cases. Worse, they couldn't afford the monster visa fees a few countries required. As soon as Hilde said, "Finally, the dam broke and the DOMINican Republic offered us asylum," we had our answer. What a way to express gratitude!

Her answer to our next question intrigued us as well. Why, after more than a decade of safe, even comfortable years in the Dominican Republic—where Erwin's work was flourishing, and Hilde began translating and lecturing at the university— did they decide, as few Jews would, to return to Germany in 1954? "You can't think, much less write, in a language while exiled away from where it is most spoken," she said plaintively. I was reminded that Conrad knew he had to learn English or return to Poland. A sudden, far-away look crossed Hilde's face. She rose slowly and held her arms out akimbo, which we took as an invitation to link ours with hers as she sped along.

"Remind me," she went on, "what poems of mine you want to ask about so I can start thinking about them on the way back to the house." When I tore out the page of my journal that listed the half dozen poems we'd chosen, we were relieved she smiled warmly after reviewing them. Although she'd already published four collections, it was her first, "*Nur eine Rose als Stütze* (Only a Rose for Support), that most captivated us, as it had legions of readers ever since it appeared in 1959. It had become something of a sensation, given its plainspoken diction and virtual absence of metaphor. To give the reader an idea of its ways, here it is:

ONLY A ROSE FOR SUPPORT

I make myself a room in the air
among the acrobats and birds:
my bed on the trapeze of feelings
like a nest in the wind
on the outermost tip of the branch.

I buy a blanket of the most delicate wool
of gently shorn sheep, which
like gleaming clouds
move across the solid earth
in the moonlight.

I close my eyes and wrap myself
in the fleece of the dependable animals.
I want to feel the sand under their tiny hooves
and the click of the latch,
closing the stall door at night.

But I'm lying in bird feathers, rocked high
    into the void.
I'm dizzy. I don't fall asleep.
My hand
reaches for something to grasp and finds
only a rose for support.

2

By the time we were comfortably seated back in her studio,
we'd laid out the contours of the anthology project. Our emphasis
was on questions we hoped poets would be willing to address for
a relatively unsophisticated audience of college students taking
upper-level German courses. "Yes, yes, now I recall from your
initial inquiry," she said, "how I was taken by that pedagogical
slant. I've also been thinking of an anthology of contemporary
German poems, whose authors I'd invite to comment on their
ways with the material; and also asking literary critics to comment
on the poems, side by side with authors' comments." We quickly

placed an early order for a copy![2]

It was clear we overstepped when asking her what poets she might include, though she let slip that "of course, Nelly Sachs, my dear sister-poet, would be a reasonable hunch." We'd heard that they were engaged in a correspondence that would make poetic-history, as one critic couched it, if it were ever published.[3] Hilde wondered if we were also on our way to visit Sachs. Alas, she never responded to our inquiry, nor had Ingeborg Bachmann, whom Hilde also asked about.

To this day, David and I regret never having gotten around to publishing the textbook we based our grant application on, though Oberlin's understanding president was quite forgiving, allowing as how there "were other fruits" harvested, e.g. the many translations we undertook and published, the stimuli to our teaching, and "who knows what else might issue down your roads" he said when we went to confession. Launching *Field*, and the Field Translation Series a few years later, topped his list. Much worse, precious few notes remain of all the conversations we had, quite aside from our questions, and answers from the likes of Domin, Grass, Brambach, Eich, Aichinger, Krolow, Heißenbüttel, and Celan. It is to weep …

3

As with other poets we visited, we peppered Hilda with questions about the poems we'd selected, to help us frame questions to pose in the textbook. Hilde, who spoke so fast it

---

2 *Doppelinterpretationen*, her epoch-making anthology, was published in 1966, a year or so after our visit.

3 The correspondence has been published (2016), albeit ten years after Domin's death.

would have taxed a stenographer to record it all, finally said, "Enough already, let's get you a memorable meal at my favorite restaurant before you depart. I trust you won't get seasick on the little ferry we'll take up the Neckar a little." There on the restaurant's menu was "Zander," the name of my high school German teacher. I knew it meant "pike," not a fish I'd normally eat. When Hilde noticed I was having trouble deciding what to order, she got me blabbing about how I'd started in on German at all, centering on Herr Zander's spell over me. David sat by so patiently I still owe him big-time.

When Hilde insisted on making her way back to her house alone, we sensed we'd used up our welcome. We parted on a warm note: she would likely be touring German institutions in the States in the near future and joked that'd be pay-back time for her hospitality. Voilà, some years later, John Kurtz, the German Department chairman, was able to get the Max Kade Foundation to underwrite Hilde's appearance at Oberlin. To this day, some students who were present at her reading and I joke about the reading she gave. "Sorry, but you've not been listening closely enough so I shall have to recite the poem again," she said piercingly after introducing the first poem, sending a shock-wave through the drowsy late-afternoon crowd.

When she finished intoning the second poem, someone shouted "Again!" She smiled broadly and launched it again; and continued repeating every poem till she got to the last poem. To thunderous applause, she recited "Nur eine Rose als Stütze" three times. Numbers of us could leave reciting it as well.

At the reception, I asked if she'd had time to look in on Dorothy's red shoes at the Smithsonian. "Alas, no. But one must always have something to live for."

Jams & Jellies:
Remembering Miroslav Holub

I

"WHERE are the jams & jellies, please?"

Those were the first words Miroslav said when we got to the IGA in Oberlin, our first stop after I picked him up at the airport in Cleveland. I'd prepared Dave the owner with a quick rundown of "Dr." Holub's considerable CV. Dave always seemed flattered that persons of some academic repute were among his customers, so I played to that bent. Bowing slightly, Dave led us to an aisle which he'd assured was stocked with the finest products available worldwide.

"So," Miroslav went on, "Where is Prague's famous apricot jam, and I'd also be interested in mulberry jelly from Pilsen, where I was born." Taking in Miroslav's rumpled suit, registering his frayed shirt collar, Dave's stare made it down to Miroslav's red shoes caked with dust. No one spoke for a loud moment. Then Miroslav, his drawn expression clouded by the long plane ride from Prague, finally muttered he'd better get on with some shopping before he collapsed. Dave stuttered, pledging he'd soon have many jams and jellies from Czechoslovakia on the shelf, and promised two free jars as a welcoming gift.

"How nice," Miroslav said, "I'll have the mice at Professor Young's scratch you out something of a thank you note!" Unsure he was joking, Dave's expression turned goofy and he scurried off. While I waited up front, Miroslav quickly plucked things off the shelves, topping his cart, and paid with a crisp $100 note he'd had to order from his bank in Prague months before departing. To our amusement the clerk held the bill up to the light as if candling an egg.

Eager to baptize his new international license, Miroslav asked to drive my car on to 220 Shipherd Circle, the Youngs' residence he would be renting for the semester, while they were off on sabbatical in London. Having coaxed some grant money out of a foundation, I'd traveled to Prague the previous summer to begin working with Miroslav on translating his poems, which we eventually published in our newly established translation series.[1] At that time, I'd also managed to persuade him to take a turn as Playwright-in-Residence for the spring semester, 1979. When someone on the hiring committee recalled that Ted Hughes once prophesied Miroslav would win Nobels for biology and literature in the same year, I quickly concluded my pitch. All hands shot up when a vote was called.

2

While I brewed a pot of tea before showing Miroslav around the Young's house and lovely grounds, Plum Creek rippling along down the back slope, the acreage crowned by splendid trees, Miroslav made his way to the master bedroom to unpack. Suddenly I heard his throaty laugh: "Come see all my new clothes!" He was already modeling one of David Young's sports jackets in the mirror, patting it down in places where it didn't quite sit right. I knew he always traveled light, and had planned

---

1 *Poems of Miroslav Holub: Sagittal Section* (co-translated by Dana Hábová & Stuart Friebert; Field Translation Series, No. 3).

on taking him to the local haberdashery. Jitka, his beloved wife, had begged me to see he'd be outfitted "properly" in respectful, Oberlinian fashion. "Please challenge where necessary his notion of "well-dressed," she'd written in a firm hand. While I sat on the bed, Miroslav methodically worked his way through whatever was hanging in the closet, setting just a few garments off to the side he wouldn't dare show up in, he grinned, because Jitka would somehow know he'd "regressed yet again."

The weekend before us, which would allow Miroslav to soldier through jet-lag and all, I proposed taking in *Invasion of the Body Snatchers*, which was playing at the Apollo downtown. Knowing of his delight regarding all manner of science-fiction flicks, I suspected he might even want to see it twice. What surprised, even shocked me, was later learning that the film had so spooked him he didn't get a good night's sleep for days: he was accustomed to leaving drapes open to enjoy images of the night sky before drifting off. Fog descending over the Youngs' back sward seemed to sprout alive with "pods" from the film, which jolted Miroslav out of bed.[2]

Having visited Miroslav at his clinic in Prague, I knew the first thing he'd do as soon as we wandered back to the kitchen to unload the groceries: he took out a package of little paper cups he'd managed to find in the IGA's bakery section and lined them up on the counter. Then he spooned an assortment of the jams and jellies he'd bought into them before swearing me to secrecy: "You must never tell the Youngs of my little game. People do not like to think their houses are havens for mice."

Having put to death many a mouse in the course of his research, he couldn't do enough to try to make it up to "our distant little cousins," he said with something of a heavy heart. I'd learned not to joke about it, having witnessed Miroslav's

---

2   Thanks to David Young for recalling Miroslav's reaction to the film, to which I must have taken him.

devotion to his beloved nude mice, whose furless skin could be inflicted with several cancers at the same time, given their severely compromised immune system. If you Google his considerable body of scientific papers, don't overlook his team's work on the omentum, one of our largest but least understood organs. He was especially gifted in helping develop drugs to suppress rejection mechanisms in transplant recipients, and Czech immunologists were leading the way to calming the body's reactions down when foreign matter invaded.

In fact, another major reason for inviting him to Oberlin was my expectation the science faculty would also want to take advantage of his contributions to the emerging field of transplantation protocols and ethics. I'd begged Miroslav to lug along a collection of slides to reference in his work, hoping to interest science colleagues in co-sponsoring a lecture; but I was surprised, not to say dismayed, that with the exception of David Egloff, a biologist, no one else would sign on to co-sponsoring.

Nonetheless, when Miroslav agreed to lecture anyway, I sent invitations to every science colleague as well as to other institutions in the area. It was soon clear the small auditorium wasn't large enough to collect the crowd. Folks traveled from Cleveland and elsewhere to attend, and several scientists who followed Miroslav's publications drove over from Pittsburgh.

When Miroslav ended his electrifying talk — during which we learned that the omentum also seems to preserve evidence of any major invasions from diphtheria to measles and thus can be read like a map of what's befallen the body — a number of the science colleagues, who'd not been interested in co-sponsoring the lecture, also lined up to pump his hand.

3

Before the semester began in earnest, Miroslav and I spent a few heavy-duty days going over the range of his duties and courses—he'd also agreed to teach the intermediate poetry workshop as well as supervise advanced writing projects in any genre—and ancillary obligations he'd be responsible for as Playwright-in-Residence. His incisive questions made me realize we ought to review a number of procedures too firmly in place; just one more benefit from having someone aboard from another discipline altogether, not to mention someone with Miroslav's acuity and investigative habits. Inasmuch as he'd never taught writing, even questioned whether or not it was teachable at all, his reactions and responses over the course of the semester were sure to be a valuable sounding board at the next departmental-review deliberations.

One of his many lasting legacies is what students have affectionately come to call "Laws According to MH"; e.g. "You are only a poet when writing a poem"; "No title, no read"; "Plays must end one second sooner than we want them to"; "We hope Othello might not strangle Desdemona in the next performance"; "Write 1000 pages, of drivel, whatever, before you show me a single phoneme"; and my favorite, which I quoted often during my teaching days, "If your roommate likes it but I don't, please sign up to work with her from now on" …

One unforgettable evening while I visited Miroslav in Prague the previous summer, he whisked me off to a roadside bar outside Prague to witness plays by Havel, Beckett, and him. They were so primitively staged, the bar darkened to the blackest black by heavy drapes, that everything could be disappeared in a flash if sirens were heard approaching. I resolved at the time to stage a series of them. But what better time than at the end of Miroslav's stay to mount a number of his one-acts, mostly written while Czechoslovakia was being trampled by Russian boots, and nothing he wrote was published except via Samizdat?

Typically "Miroslavian," he couldn't stop hugging the student actors for how deeply they'd "assayed" his texts, especially commending a student nicknamed "Tree" for his way of sending roots deep into the undergrowth. Slapping "Tree" on the back, Miroslav said he'd like to smuggle him into Czechoslovakia to join his theater's ensemble. To this day I tease "Tree" about a major lost opportunity.

4

"You know I must do some shopping at Value City on the way to the airport," he said, the day before he was to depart. "So, let's please leave an hour earlier than planned. Besides, it'll be a nice bookend to stopping at the IGA when I first arrived, don't you think?" he grinned.

But of course! I'd forgotten that anytime he'd travel the world, he would carry an extra bag to fill with expected gifts for family and friends. When we parked at Value City, on the outskirts of Elyria, Miroslav asked me to repeat the story I'd once regaled him with, bringing tears to his eyes. In a book on amnesiacs, I'd read that Sherwood Anderson—whose work Miroslav cherished—had once owned a paint manufacturing company in Elyria, but for unknown reasons—amnesia having set in?—was said to get up one day, close the door quietly behind him, and proceed to walk the railroad tracks east to Cleveland. Somehow he made his way to a pharmacy, where, disheveled and distraught, it was clear he had no idea who he was. Subsequently, he was treated in a psychiatric clinic. Released, he divorced his wife and left his family to join a writing group in Chicago, where he launched his writing career in earnest. The *Elyria Chronicle*'s headline, when Anderson died, just made mention of his work at the paint company, with nary a word about his by then illustrious writing career. I've rarely seen another human as giddy as Miroslav when crooning the headline: "WELL-KNOWN PAINT MANUFACTURER DIES!"

Motioning me to guide one cart while he pushed the other through the aisles at Value City, he made a beeline for where jeans of all sorts were heaped up on splintery wooden counters. Jeans were still the most desired clothing he could gift, especially for the younger Czech generation, so he plopped a dozen pairs into our carts without so much as a glance at sizes. When I teased him about possibly returning with poor fits, he reminded me of "the Czech existential condition: We accept what's available, and try to disguise our displeasure. Remember when I took you shopping for our famous soccer teams' shirts for your kids at Prague's best department store?" he said. The long table on the fourth floor, to which we'd made our way through clouds of dust, was domed with swells of shirts all sized SMALL. At first, my kids were disappointed because even after many a wash and stretch they wouldn't fit. Over the years they've become prize possessions.

When he looked out from the plane's window right before take-off, he gave a little wave, the kind European kids make, fingers curled back.

Late Poems

BORN ON

The twelfth of July, like Neruda, wouldn't
you also need to see *Il Postino* to start

another year off on high, given you'll never
make it up Machu Picchu on your broken hip?

Come winter, however, can get to a park like
Stefan George's, my other birthday buddy,

whose poems I defended liking more than Rilke's
in that life-changing seminar up in Bascom Hall,

highest elevation in Madison, in front of which
Abe Lincoln sits on a massive throne-like chair,

who shouldn't be in this because he wasn't born
when we were, but into whose lap I climbed after

taking some whacks from the Rilkean gang, urged
on by Professor H … Thank The One Above Melitta

Gerhard came along, who'd escaped the Nazis &
after retiring from an illustrious scholarly career

settled in Cambridge, where she befriended a few
of us underlings in Harvard's German Department,

lit a candle before George's picture on her mantle,
and swore us into The SG Society. If my mother

were alive, she'd have made SG patches for our
parkas, and off we'd have trudged into the snow,

crooning "Come into the park said to be dead …"
Bernd Heinrich would understand, whose winter

tales are a match for *The Winter's Tale*, in which
I'd have cast Danny Kaye as the clown, but stopped

directing after putting on *Wozzeck* with students
at Oberlin in my salad days; "when I was green in

judgment, cold in blood." Remember poor Wozzeck
baying, "The moon's a bloody iron," before he killed

Maria? Spent the longest time working with the army's
actor-doc, examining Wozzeck, whose pulse he found

"small, hard, hopping." My pulse is hopping now, sitting
on my 88th milestone, because I'm looking up at turgid

clouds trying to give me a nephology lesson, but all I
get is a headache without the giddiness it used to leave

behind for days. The headache's because who can get
over Massimo Troisi finding ways to finish *Il Postino*

knowing he was dying? I try to warn him every time
I watch the film; and somehow hope, as I always do,

that next time Othello will not strangle Desdemona,
and the postman's coming son will not be fatherless.

WOLF BIRDS

—for Gary, who knows BH

Bernd Heinrich calls ravens, who partner
with wolves to hunt, calling from on high

till wolves open other mammals' bodies,
then eat side by side, & whose artful wings

can be heard flapping at some distance, for
instance by us now in our tent, sleeping bags

zippered up to chins, straining to catch last
faint murmurs before our eyelids flutter: on

to REM sleep! Better at remembering dreams,
Gary opens some over morning coffee to my

confusion: something about Jung, collective
consciousness, things circling things, touching

spines, sticking out of flesh, some law of nature
to answer to. I stammer that the laws of nature

have reversed at times. Gary frowns, knows I love
trying his patience, say anything to be contrary—

best thing, change the subject: Remember the old
Algonquin tale, ravens flew and flew till reaching

the end of time? Well, we have the honor of not
understanding that either … Don't know about you,

he says, diving into his waders, blowing a smoke-ring,
but I need to find a good hole to cast from in the river.

SEA FOAM

Recall Aphrodite and Venus sprang from some,
according to Hesiod the results of Uranus' genitals
having been lopped off by Cronus, pitched into
the sea; but alas not depicted in any paintings,
not even Botticelli's *The Birth of Venus.* "Foam,"
I read, may not be found anywhere else except
on Earth, where wind blows across open water
to make some, one moment stopping to spritz,
the next vortexing around till finding itself gods
know where. Mist around our bow now, while
we slip into rain gear for what will turn out to be
our last fishing trip together. Readying our rods,
he keeps staring the line along. It's getting harder
to guess his next move. One thing's for sure, he's
never been quite okay about my going off to books,
ignoring his advice to pick up a trade along the way
just in case. One thing's certain. Not much longer
till he complains mother's too hard on him, won't,
you know … Oh, Dad! I want to scream but of
course never can; want to ferry him off to some
Greek island for some unknown fish, see the sea
foam as it never does elsewhere, so thick it coats
your face, bouncing on waves to curl your hair,
shake a fist at the heavens and shout, More, more!

Instead, I hold out a fingertip to him, hoping he'll
point one back, see if there's any current between us.
He gives me one of those "for chrissake let's have more
than a finger" looks, holds out a soft hand so when I
respond to the minimal pressure mine slips right through.

PFEILSTORCH

A.k.a. arrow-stork, which on a pleasant day
in the merry month of May, 1822, Count Christian

Ludwig von Bothmer shot down on the grounds
of his castle in Klütz, Germany, startled to see

a lengthy wooden spear impaling it, which a local
scholar deduced found its mark from "the hands of

an African!" Imagine flying for all the many thousands
of miles to Europe, let alone so burdened. At that point

worldwide wisdom believed, to quote Charles Morton
in 1703, they "miraculously dropped down from Heaven."

At the inn I'd frequent, just outside of Darmstadt where
Karl Krolow resided, whenever he said, "Come on over

the pond, I have time now," to perfect translations he
allowed me to publish for more than thirty years, two

storks built a nest halfway covering the tiled roof during
my last visit. While we sat and worked, every so often

Krolow poured us a jigger of his best cognac to toast
the storks on the inn's roof. "They augur good fortune,

even if we mess up the consequences will be slight," he said.
Alas, mess up I did, let 6 typos escape into the collection,

which appeared after Krolow died. Many years later, though
remorse has since yielded to a gentle melancholy, every time

I catch myself doodling, a tiny arrow keeps emerging from
all the storks I can't stop assembling, which augurs what?

THALWEG

"The line defining the lowest points
along a river bed or valley," I read,
"which lawyers employ to test legal
property limits, to hydrologists a line
of fastest, deepest water to a river,
underwater and invisible." I came

to it through German studies: "Weg"
is cognate with "way," "Thal" with "dale,"
which we'd bust out singing — "Over hill,
over dale …" on hikes in the Harz Mountains,
looking for the hut on whose wall Goethe
is said to have carved his most famous poem:

"Über allen Gipfeln // ist Ruh // in allen Wipfeln
// spürest du // kaum einen Hauch" … While
he was able to visit the hut fifty years later, just
before he died, and cried, it has since disappeared.
Can't help thinking when he found it there was
nothing else for him to look for, and was perhaps

afraid, yes, really seemed to be afraid to run his
fingers over it one last time. And what about our
walking up and down the ground for many an hour?
Back at the Technische Hochschule, we were told
we looked a little thinner, and soon a rumor spread
we had come down with something communicable.

EMILY, AGAIN

"I hope you love birds, too.
It is economical. It saves going
to heaven," she wrote, I imagine,

in the window's rime, her finger
ringless from living so separately,
but not afraid of God. In the evening,

in her bedroom listening to someone
playing a fiddle below, voices chattering,
she turned to tea and crackers, sat there

rather a long time after the company left,
listening to the night's last notes, likely
an owl hooting, beginning its hunting.

In the baseboard, Emmaline would be safe,
but not any of her cousins tunneling under
snow, whose urine any owl worth its hoot

sees; not to mention its magnetoreception,
resulting in entanglement, more difficult to
disengage from than most fervent desires.

ON BEING SCHOPENHAUER

Who, we read, would daily walk
his poodle, then practice the fiddle.

To steady himself, methinks, to hold
forth at the University in Berlin, where

he was allowed to docent, provided
at least three students would enroll

in the course proposed. Imagine
intentionally scheduling "My Intro

to Philosophy" at exactly the same
time Hegel held forth in the largest

lecture hall, filled to the brim given
his reputation and theatrical ways

of engaging anyone with a brain.
Well, we know three students did

in fact enroll in Arthur's seminar
the first semester (have studied

him enough myself to fancy first-
naming him); but fewer the second,

so he was forced to fiddle away in
private thereafter, take some anger

out on his poor poodle, whose cries
disturbed a neighbor. Revenge came,

however, quite soon, as Hegel perished
in the Plague that swept Berlin while

Arthur drank to his own health, perhaps
plucking out The Dance of Death as well.

THE THINGS HE SAYS

Inasmuch as rivers don't run straight more than
ten times their width, the one we're fishing must

have been altered by human hands, which perhaps
explains why the bass Whitt releases has ugly rusty

spots on its fins. I'm an octo now, Whitt adds "pus,"
because I retreat more and more into my hidey hole,

solitary to a point of worry. "Gloomier than you used
to be," Whitt says, my buddy going way back, who's

on my case when I pretend he took a better bend in
life's stream: "Don't mess with me, you were born to

compete. Me, I never gave a shit, just wanted enough
so's I could live near water, catch enough fish to eat,

keep the suffering and remorse to a minimum the rest
of you were headed for, like that hole there!" he yells,

shoving me aside in the nick of time. When we were kids,
he'd taught me water flowing over an underwater ridge

drops suddenly, speeds way up, then falls down lower than
the water around, kills you just like that between the flows.

AN ACCOUNT

Prized by trout especially, the mayfly
spends its first two years in just the right
mud, then goes airborne for only a day,
doesn't even have time for a stomach!

A subject for nearly a month, to get me
through what I'm going through, I try to
learn everything remotely possible about
its why and wherefores, can't sit still

for a moment, keep rubbing my hands.
When Whitt comes by, curious, I get
childishly impatient, pour him just one
drink, turn his chair toward the door.

He crosses his legs one way, then another.
"They're sure to catch you more fish," he
says, "Once you know how to present them."
I nod the way you would to agree quickly,

cough dramatically, hope he'll get the hint.
Suddenly he gets up, surging like a wave,
"What I've got to say to you, it's not that
simple, I just don't want to know you much

longer." Deep silence sets in, pooling around
my chair, in which a mayfly takes a last sip
before upending on a ripple, just as a trout
below, no break to the surface, dimples it down.

EVEN SLIGHTLY

When Tristan Gooley writes, "Anything
that lands on water will bend the surface
skin slightly, even the tiniest of insects on
a clear, shallow pond will create a gorgeous
pattern on the bottom: tiny, bright pools
of sunshine, one for each of its tiny feet,"
I pay attention, because I've been a poor
fly-caster, never catch much while others
fill their creels. Oh, I follow their tips about
which fly to apply, but now realize my flies
land too hard, the way my son's plane would
have problems if he didn't bring it down just
so. Thinking of him now, off on Guam, not
exactly out of harm's way, though he assures
it's still pretty much business as usual; they'd
know if things were getting really dicey, just
look to the surrounding waters for build-up,
sudden "activity" — "No worries yet, Dad."

A parent himself, he must have worries though
for his own son in these turbulent times, how
not to think and feel things are not worsening.
Of course, I should hold my tongue, not borrow
trouble from tomorrow, as the saying goes, and
Charles Schulz comes to mind: "Don't worry about
the world coming to an end today, for it's already
tomorrow in Australia" (not that far from Guam).
When I turn to Matthew 6:34, I realize how much
that seems negative can also be seen positively,
so it's back to "tiny bright pools of sunshine," to
"accentuate the positive, eliminate the negative,"

find that old Bing Crosby recording, raise a jigger
to Johnny Mercer of course for "listen to children,"
who in our case is Master Felix, about to turn eleven,
on course with all children to atone for our sins.

COWBELLY

Look it up: "Patches of superfine silt
in the slowest part of rivers." Can't help
thinking Virginia's last steps might have
sunk pleasurably and brought her to

a stop till the stones pressed against
a hip, jolting her on down to the bed.
A life spent looking at things less simply
than the rest of us, once tuned up won't

stop playing, is how my high-strumming
pal put it. He'd written her a number of
songs she'll never hear. Hiking a river in
Massachusetts another lifetime ago —

we were both teaching at Mt. Holyoke,
and lived in Dickinson House — we joked
our next jobs should deposit us in Woolf
House, given our pledge to read every

single phoneme she ever published, which
journey began with Night and Day, an early
novel we were on a mission to elevate to
Conference-Heights on the academic trail.

So hard to anticipate the twists and turns
of mind without her signature sharpness,
perhaps it's best to pull our caps down over
our brows, pick up a stone, skip it across

the divide to her side, then whirl and stride
back up the path, hoping to see a rook free
of the flock in *Night and Day*, perching on
a cow's backside over there by the fence.

JEWFISH

So called for unknown reasons,
my etymological dictionary says,

but I can think of a few. Beady eyes,
body half as wide as long, thick skin,

tons of teeth, but swallows prey whole,
a.k.a. goliath grouper, can pack 1000+

pounds on its 8-foot body, humans and
large sharks its only predators. Females

squirt some fifty million eggs out for sperm
to join the party, overwrought to the point

of madness. Do you know where this is going?
I sure don't, have washed my face with a bar

of soap my cousin somehow saved from his
Death Camp days, gargled to quiet my throat,

and finally stopped screaming after throwing
Bettelheim's *The Informed Heart* at the wall.

Must email my German pal, a foremost Arendt
scholar, Please, Thomas, what exactly did she mean?

Not to mention why is anybody suggesting arming
school teachers is a good idea? That'd be a dreadful

life, standing at the blackboard with your back to
the class, your Glock holstered, hurting your hip,

impossible not to imagine a hallway duel, impossible
to think you could avoid it if. The veins in your throat

swell, your nostrils quiver. Ever get called a queer fish?
Well, I did, a month ago at the P.O., by a guy who can't

shake your hand without crunching down. I screamed
so loud — arthritic fingers stick out every which way —

Tony the cop, who happened to be outside, came
bursting in, his gun cocked. We sort of joke about it

now, tell each other things are never going to get so
out of hand in our little burg, *feste,* Luther might say.

Ever read what he wrote about Jews? I'd tell him I was
ready to hear anything he had to say, if he agreed to say

nothing ever again about Jews, offer to take him fishing,
promise I'd make him an unforgettable meal he could

say the Blessing at. We'd start off with gramma's recipe
for gefilte fish: "Stupidoll," she'd coo, just bring me back

some Jewfish filets, remember to sharpen your penknife!"

ON THE BEACH

The chart I'm looking at for Lake Erie
has many an "S" — for sand; many an
"Sh" — for shells; a forest of "Wd" —
for weeds, "M" — for mud all over;
and "Oz" — for ooze, critical, I read,
"for any vessel dropping anchor."

My mate's swimming below, while
I'm up on a bluff tracking her wake,
a steady mix of crawl, side & breast
stroke, before I lose her because she's
disappeared for a stretch till bubbling
up to float, signaling she's okay. Not

that I worry. She swam out of the womb,
we joke, always dreaming of the next swim,
grew up crisscrossing vacation lakes. When
we finally had to stop booking our favorite
cabin on Loon Lake in northern Ontario —
too old and cold, we jingled — she was resigned

to adapting to Erie's changing habits, closely
monitors the bacteria count before we pack
for a day at the beach. Eventually, all lakes
will fill in long after we're gone, closing, as
Tranströmer said, their windows into Earth

the ooze building up so nothing anchoring in it
will ever be able to set off again, rendering all
our enterprises luckless, to rhyme with muck.

YOKOI'S CAVES

   — for Kazu

Owe my grandson & his Cub Scout troop, taken
on a tour, knowledge of Shoichi Yokoi's hideouts
on Guam, now registered Historic Places, visited

even by Japanese tourists to honor a National
Hero, a sergeant in the Imperial Japanese Army
during WW II, told to prefer death to disgrace of

getting captured, but captured he finally was, in
1972, by two Chamorros checking their fish traps,
whom he begged to kill him but was fed instead

before they turned him over to the Commissioner,
in clothes of hibiscus bark fiber he'd woven, having
been a tailor before the war. Back home, his first words

"It is an embarrassment that I return," he'd saved his rusty
rifle to gift Emperor Hirohito, lived many a year more only
to suffer nightmares of being chased by the enemy. Such

things are possible, I read and weep. May my grandson
work his way out of all danger with such temerity, but by
the time he is old, remember his past with some pride.

KOSSUTH'S HAT

You perhaps know it as a slouch hat,
flat-topped crown, rolled brim, could be
seen on Union and Confederate heads alike,

later sported by Teddy Roosevelt and his
rough riders, now worn by half of Australia;
but the one I've been looking for everywhere

Lajos Kossuth wore and signed for my grampa,
which both shared wearing in the last parade
Kossuth led for social justice and workers' rights

in Budapest before he fled to America, while
grampa fled to London to escape military service.
Apprenticed to a tailor, soon sewing with such

confidence, he could follow his hero to America,
tailoring away for years till Eugene Debs so favored
grampa's vests the future seemed bright enough

to sire four sons, whom gramma mostly had to raise,
because grampa relaxed playing pinochle with many
other Milwaukee Socialists at Steuben Hall, on whose

thumb-tacked wall an anonymous poem might still
hang; from The Cambridge Chronicle, March, 1852,
which begins, "Thou, too, call on, O Ship of State!
    Thou, too, stick on, O Kossuth's pelt!"

CALIDARIUS

"Legendary bird the color of snow
the Romans thought able to take

on someone's sickness, fly away,
expel it," leaving the soul healed,

I read, buried in my couch, nowhere
near Duffy's farm; Robert Bly said to

be sliding into oblivion, Jim Wright dead,
Franz now too, so no more midnight calls:

"How's my boy doin'?" "Fine, Jim," I'd lie
at times, the image of young Franz lying

in the middle of the street frozen in my
mind's eye, snow falling, covering him in

down, while I tried not to make a sound, so
my own kids wouldn't wake, hushed down

the back stairs, rushed to gather Franz up,
get him back to his digs, make sure he'd keep

sleeping naturally before I retreated. Back up
in my study, I looked down to the angel shape

he'd somehow made, drew the heavy window
drapes, threw myself down on the floor, pulled

the afghan off the couch, but could not coax
myself to sleep till Calidarius came back for me.

SNEAKER MALES

After a male has courted a female
unsuccessfully, an SM flies in to score,
said behavior found in birds, insects,
and other animals like the cuttlefish,
the master among them all, which can
convert its skin to a "manly, colorful
display to impress the female," I read.
And imagine doing that on just one side
of your body facing her, on the other side
of which he "sports a female's coloration,
so other males waste time impressing him."

If only I could get back to the North Sea,
in whose sublittoral depths cuttlefish thrive,
I'd perhaps have more to add to their story,
but I'm tired out from changing my colors
over the years, forever restless, not troubling
myself about my own nothingness, the flesh
hanging ever lower from my neck and throat,
as close as a human could come to resembling
a wattlebird no other male's wasted his time on.

Except for that moment in the men's bathroom
at the faculty club in Madison, where I was able
to have a room as a graduate assistant, and my
major professor lived in a suite at the other end
of the corridor, so we'd sometimes meet shaving
mornings at adjacent washbowls. "Next time you
find yourself chasing a bat down toward my door"
—near Lake Mendota, Madison was often chock-
a-block with them—"Why not knock so we can

have a sherry together, something like that?" is
all he said or had to say. I took no offence.

DO NOT JEST

Were you there when the Cossacks
caught sturgeon with baited hooks

tethered to a tree or sometimes tied
to an ox? Well, I wasn't either but I

do remember sawing through the ice
on Lake Winnebago, instructed by

my grampa in the art of making holes
he'd drop bait into, chunks of herring

to attract the lake's abundant sturgeon
in the 1930s, while he'd clutch a spear

hoping a "shadow" would glide into view,
yell at me to make sure the 100 lb. test

line attached was spooled just so, would
not tangle when he let the spear fly. Luck

would get us enough filets gramma would
churn and turn into gefilte fish I couldn't

stomach, while she wagged her finger: You
wouldn't be here unless I escaped Cossacks

thundering down our shtetl's muddy ruts by
the hair on my chin now. Whenever grampa

so much as dared suggest she might consider
trimming it back a bit, she'd spear him with

a sharp glance, bite into a chunk of sturgeon,
her chin disappearing in the gelatinous broth.

CLOUDY

—for Don Vreuls

We called it, the small blue marble,
but thanks to Apollo 8's astronauts
an oasis in space's blackness aka Earth.

Down on our scabby knees those summers
during WW II, drawing circles in the sand
to set up our mibby matches, we'd only look

up at the sky when the sirens wailed, which
they'd do periodically when the headlines
scared us, another setback thanks to Rommel

outsmarting Monty, another awful battle to
regain an island in the Pacific. Augie's crooked
finger let him grip his shooter better so he'd

eventually always plunk more of our mibbies,
send them scuttling out of the circle, where he'd
pluck them up, stash them in the little burlap sack

we all stored our gains in, which our mothers
made for us in their sewing circle. Augie's & mine
died the youngest, which kept us bonded, in touch

till the other day. The obit said the plane he'd built
in the field behind his lot lost altitude so fast for
as yet unknown reasons he couldn't counteract.

We'd joked now & then we'd have made problematic
astronauts, if we'd somehow managed to make it
through the program, because our cloudies always

had so many nicks they'd turn black; something
about their insides taking on more carbon atoms,
a physicist pal hunched. Pray, what shall play, now?

PAREIDOLIA

Our brains can't help it, I read, "Find patterns
and ascribe meaning where there may be none."
If I practiced folk etymology, that'd morph into
paranoia by and by. Not alas like Smart's, practiced
or not, who knows? Unless, like Ivan Blatný, more
recently institutionalized in Bixley, you managed
to start writing and never stopped till 280,000
poems dripped from your pen. Hard to imagine even
in all his thirty plus years there, when he wasn't busy
running in the woods looking for other seeds to plant.

If I ever made it to Ipswich, Bixley staff would soon
confirm my paranoia. I'd beg to be assigned to Ivan's
old room, hope to breathe whatever air left he did,
sleep longer than usual to start with. How he guarded
his rest! Was that the key? Insomnia grips your body
with iron fingers, while attending visions invent other
ways of tormenting you. Each night's bout seems like
the last limit. Hah. OK, all right, my verdict's light, so
I lose my temper easily, so? Blatný endured way worse,
so enough of trivial complaints. I'm readily seen when
I'm not writing, nowhere close to his "Will you see me
if I'm no longer writing?" Actually, my good man, WON'T!

AN ODE TO GLASSES

That's a hawk, oops, a squirrel.
You realize this is more serious.

Out after dark, the path leading
nowhere in particular, I'm more

and more confused by old sights,
lately scarcely able to focus for long.

Cataracts, Doc Austin says, asks if
he can pray over me before he squints

& fires the laser. (A friend shot up,
"Absolutely not," she yelled, dragged

herself off the gurney.) But I comply,
feel pity. Word is his brain's tumoring,

will soon retire him. He's proud he can
send you off without glasses. ("Why bother

with them anymore?") Not able to confess
my family's told me they make me look

better, more serious, I blurt out sheer
nonsense, cross myself wrong: "The Lord

is my shepherd, I shall wear glasses,
don't be downhearted my good man!"

His eyes cross when I shake his hand.

BOTTOM-UP ATTENTION

Courtesy of our reptilian brain, I read,
so whether we want to or not we'll hear

danger afoot even if focused on something
top-down attention serves up. If your great

great great great great great great forefather
hadn't heard the lion in the bush for beating

his drum, you'd never have sung a song by
the camp fire. My father, who worked better

with his hands than his head, easily caught
fish I could only dream of, so we always ate.

"Wish I could lie around like that, just read,"
he'd grumble, when Mom whispered, "Shush,

he's studying." Stupidly, I thought she loved
me more, till he pressed my hand four times

with last strength, while he lay dying. "Do I
love you," he whispered, after I mopped his

brow. Silence. Then "Yes, I do." Silence. Then
"How Much?" Silence. One last press. "Ohhh."

HIBAKU JUMOKU

   — lit. "bombed trees"

"You must see them," Akihirio Takahashi,
one ear crushed, hands clawed up, nails
blackened, I read, said to Ariel Dorfman,

"You must see the gingkos, they're survivors."
Just six left in Hiroshima, their barks scorched,
grew new shoots and buds the first spring after

the blast. Dorfman, who knew from blasts on
the other side of the globe, said he could only

wheeze. Imagine bonding over wild screams
in the dead of night, leaning your head against

the wall, clutching your hair with your hands,
remaining motionless. What do you do then?

SILENT RETREAT

Jain monks I come upon whisk
small beings from the sandy path,

wear masks to prevent inhaling
them, do not seem to show any

consciousness. They're visiting
the monastery where I'm also in

silent retreat, fix their eyes on
bread served at supper, noses

disappearing in chunks. When
my stomach rumbles, one shakes

his head, scratches his shoulder.
I screw up my face to show regret,

suddenly wish to reform my will
in accordance with their senses,

move another muscle. I slap at
something crawling up my leg.

IF

Both your daughters
Died in childbirth

Son Karl was killed
At Verdun

Son Erwin was taken
Prisoner, only to be

Executed by the Nazis
Years later for plotting

Against Hitler, your name
Was Max Planck.

ON DYING OF ATLANTO-AXIAL DISLOCATION

Aka a broken neck, we read, written across
Girolamo Zini's skull, a nineteenth century
tightrope artist from Trieste, the first exhibit
on our tour of the Mütter Museum in Philly.
When our guide rubs the back of his neck,
we all follow to the next vitrine: Andrejew
Sokoloff's considerable skull, of which he
relieved himself following the dire command
of self-emasculation by his religious order.

TOM, DICK, AND HARRY

Dick is what you might name your mockingbird
if like Thomas Jefferson you'd spent Cucillin,
Bergère & Fingal naming horses and sheepdogs.

Mimus polyglottos, many-tongued mimic, Dick,
who cost the president $10, serenaded him with
Scottish and French songs after first renditioning

the local birds, while my mother's, which cost
her $125, didn't deliver on the store's promise,
could barely emit the species harsh *tschak*! No

wonder, the autopsy showed a malformed syrinx.
Pete's Pets talked her into going with a budgie,
instead: "It'll be lots easier to care for, and it can

vocalize almost as well as the mocker; eats cheap."
So Tom was the first of dozens that kept us company
at breakfast for years, his cage left open so he could

take food from her lip, sing back whatever she sang,
make her laugh like a little girl, make it ever clearer
she was more comfortable in Tom's company, to put

it one way. The day he disappeared she ran from one
window to another, suspected I'd left the milk chute
open behind his cage. "You could have opened it,

right?" she raised her voice. I swore the door was
shut the morning minus Tom. Gramma chimed in,
"No more tears, we just go out and get Harry now!"

UNIVERSAL RIGHTS

Eleanor Roosevelt said at the U.N.
"begin in small places, close to home —
so close and so small they cannot
be seen on any maps of the world."

These stormy days some of us just
seem bent on keeping comfortable.
Some bear others a grudge, some
make ingratiating remarks, others

clench a fist, snap their heads when
I ask to pass their cart at the market.
One day, walking the square, I shout
I intend to go on singing. Yes singing,

damn it, I have a right to! The mic's
still on in the gazebo from last night's
concert on the square, so I warble
 "The longer you live, the sooner you'll

bloody well die" from an old Irish ballad.
Suddenly I have an audience: the albino
squirrel that's been drawing tourists to
town squats back on its haunches, starts

grooming itself, swaying to the tune. Tony
the cop ambles by, "You all right, buddy?
Need me to call your wife to pick you up?"
When I try telling him some of the trees

don't look so well, especially the elms, he
rolls his eyes, tips his cap to the squirrel,
and heads off to ticket more cars parked
too long. "What's to become of us now," I

try on the squirrel; and I swear it peeps out,
"I don't bite, wish folks would understand."
"Allow me to remark," I say, "I wish that'd
apply to humans in general." And weep.

"THIS TINY TOUGH SCRAP OF LIFE"

C. elegans, I read, survived Columbia's
disintegration in 2003, when the shuttle

returned to Earth, only to be dispatched
again in 2009 to the space station's lab

to study muscle development under stress
of zero gravity, alas not soon enough to save

my cousin from ALS. "It's like being whipped
so you remember it for weeks," he whispered,

his voice weaker than ever. I knew enough
not to try to jolly him anymore. The one stop

we could make near the end of the line, his
Milwaukee Brewers. They should have hired

him as Chief of Statistics. "Moneyball" was
child's play, given his ways of breaking down

the numbers to reveal ultimate outcomes. In
a moment of fervent excitement, he'd lower

his voice, breaking with impatience: "Three
cheers for passive awareness!" His mantra for

management's worst impulses. Now that he's
gone, I read more and more about disasters,

hoping for some sign of recovery, hence my
newfound affection for *C. elegans*. Think I'll

fetch some water from the muddy pond, slide
it under my microscope. Jerry would be sure

to see what I'm having trouble to, the worm no
bigger than a comma, angling off toward the sea.

OBJECT PERMANENCE

"It is a joy to be hidden, but a disaster not to be found"
    —D. W. Winnicott

Psychologists call the sudden insight
infants barely half a year old come to

that objects and people as well exist
even though they can't see them, so

of course peekaboo gives rise to glee.
"*Fort*," Freud's little grandson Ernst

crooned when he'd throw a wooden
spool attached to a piece of string out

of his playpen, then cried "Da" reeling it
back up again, while Freud watched him

for hours, sending up smoke rings from
his cigar to add to Ernst's amusement,

making copious notes for a paper he'd call
"repetition compulsion," choking off worries:

Ernst's father off at the front, his mother
ill, with not much longer to live. Suddenly,

no more "fort" and "da" in the air, Freud
looked back at Ernst, who'd laid his head

on both arms and fallen asleep. Puffing at
his cigar, breathing hard, Freud sat waiting.

PATRON OF CATS

None other than St. Gertrude, I read,
startled. So, maybe not a coincidence

that my mother's name was Gertrude!
She'd take in stray cats and later when

she was wheelchaired order my father
to feed the outsiders too nervous to risk

joining the inside clowder. Her favorite,
Molokai, she said was sheer black with

a white nose though we never saw him.
She could also disappear at times behind

a crossword, slurping another Blatz, off
to where it was impossible to follow. Over

the years, visiting less often, we were only
faintly aware of the odor of ammonia until

the house had to be scrubbed to sell, mom
and dad moved into a facility. Let us now

drink a glass to the bitter end of those days.
We placed what kittens were left crouching

under chairs and beds with neighbor children,
who pressed them against their chests, quickly

renamed them, while we slowly went back
to our own lives and opened all the windows.

SPIRIT BEAR

No, not polar! It's black
with white fur is all. If

you come upon it, I'm told
by the old Inuit guide, it'll

look puzzled at first, but
a radiant smile will follow;

a breath of something pass
between you, drawing you

closer together. Whatever you
do, do not turn your back, as

disease or at least deformity
will follow. Alas, the whole week

passes without sighting anything
remotely similar; and return I must

to my old desk in the basement of
Rice Hall, submissions to *Field* piling

up. I slit the envelopes open carefully,
tease the poems out, hope for surprise.

Alas, there are no bear poems, not even
one by Jim Dickey about the grizz he told

Dick Cavett he'd want to be eaten by; took
out a toothpick to suck on, Jim and Dick

grinning away like 1st-grade buds. When I
try writing something about the Spirit Bear

I never saw, all I see's my guide wagging his
finger, cursing. Hunger and darkness follow.

"YOU BE GOOD, SEE YOU TOMORROW, I LOVE YOU"

  —for Ute von Funcke

Alex's last words to Irene Pepperberg, his longtime pal,
before she put him back in his cage for the night, I read.

African gray parrots normally live twice as long as Alex,
who only made it to 31. We can likely barely imagine her

grief, who'd long partnered with him to prove he had brain
power right up there with chimps and toddlers, at times

beyond it seemed, for she concluded he also had a sense
of abstract ideas, could chat "with cogency and feeling."

All this inclines toward mysticism. A mind begins to ache.
We ought to know things without explanation, cry openly

when things go wrong, creatures die. Instead I'm inclined
to stamp my feet, look haggard, risk looking directly at

the sun. For all the times, I should be dead of melanoma,
or at least blind as my old professor. Here he is, coming

down the road, propped up by two canes, his nurse ready
to steady him if. Ask him how he is and he'll say, "Well,

my liver's this, my kidney's that, and my ticker's tiring,
but personally I feel *wunderbar*," then poke you in a rib

with a bony finger. "You be good, now" he says. "See you
tomorrow," I say. "I love you," he says to his nurse, aglow.

SEXY SYLLABLES

is, I read, a "real term" among ornithologists,
for male birds that use the syrinx to sing with

two different voices at once; dueting with self,
which females prefer to single-voice syllables.

Here we are walking up and down under the weft
of branches ringing with a swamp sparrow's double-

tunes, beguiling us along with the female flitting
up till she disappears. You're trying to spot her

when I fling my arms around your neck. "Whoa,
not so fast, pal," you chirp, "Till you double your

pitch!" At least you don't leave my side till dawn.
On the opposite shore the boughs are already bare.

FOR LIFE

—for Susan & Gary

After the male Andean condor lifts
his wings to dance, I read, starts to

cluck and prance, his neck inflates,
brightens to yellow, so if the female

signs on, they'll glide on thermals
for hours, nary a flap, mated for life.

Found in Translation

WHEN I first took German in high school in the '40s—along with Latin the other language one was counseled to study for a career in medicine—I began a problematic relationship with my teacher, a mysterious German emigrant, and through him with the German language itself that has divided my mind ever since, in ways I've written about over the years.[1]

Translation was still an orthodox mode of language instruction at the time, but my teacher was wise enough to limit our use of English in general, laying a foundation for fluency that has served me well to this day. Eager to please, during the German-only phases, I strove to do exactly as he preached, and practiced hard as a musician might to get all the notes right, remain in key. However, again and again I'd stray outside the lines more often than not in responses to the traditional translation exercises he assigned. Early clashes seemed to multiply until our final set-to, at which time I was taking what I thought would be my last class in German at Wisconsin State College to prepare me for any future language requirement. Alas, I had the temerity to back up my versions of texts he had me still translating, as a sort of joke but a way of remaining in touch, by running them past my college German professor, which put a sudden end to my high school teacher's rejoinders altogether. The next time I came across his name was in his obituary.

My sophomore year at WSC, spent as an exchange student in Germany, carried me off into deeper waters, farther away from any more translation efforts, as I had to concentrate on using German to keep up with my courses and maintain social interactions with staff, faculty, and fellow students, not to mention the local townspeople. Still focused on a life in science, I

---

1   Great thanks to the Wick Poetry Center/Kent State University for inviting me to teach a mini-workshop in translation in the fall of 2016, which got me thinking about my "Life in Translation" in new ways.

was jolted by the single humanities course I was obliged to take—one way we studied ancient texts called for translating some passages into modern German; or studying the language from the inside out, as Professor Karl Langosch put it. That activity soon led to writing poems I tried to court a fellow student with. She was gentle about pointing out they were sweet imitations of whatever we were studying; so that would have been that, but for Langosch's reaction to my response to an exam question. Instead of the usual "contrast & compare" essay, he offered the option of writing additional lines to a fragmented text we were studying; and for unknown reasons my "poetic" German showed enough promise for him to encourage me to keep doodling, as he put it. Even at the time I felt as if I were translating something as yet inchoate deep inside, only the tremors of which were palpable. He also challenged me to reconsider going on in science; so much so that when I returned to finish my BA I went on with German courses, which added up to a third major. This led in turn to my applying to grad school in German as well as chemistry and mathematics, thinking by summer's end I would somehow know which fork to take. A no-nonsense uncle advised, "Go where the money is. They'll take more of an interest in you than if you paid your own way." When the German Department at the University of Wisconsin/Madison offered me an assistantship—partly because of the fluency I'd acquired during the year I'd spent in Germany—and the sciences simply admitted me, my uncle's advice prevailed.

Inasmuch as we read everything in the original German in grad school, I had little reason to explore the mysteries of translation—aside from continuing to write poems in German, which I soon began trying out in English as well—a pal joked he'd soon go crazy playing Ping-Pong with himself! However, though I had chosen the literature, not the linguistics, track, something else happened when I was obliged to study phonetics, Middle High

German, then Gothic as well: I began to see and hear German and English not just as sister languages, but as twins of a sort. The linguistics courses, especially those centering on philological and cognate relationships, took us down into the phonemes, the very cells they both emerged from. Wisconsin was perhaps alone, back then, in requiring literature and linguistics concentrators to take a healthy dose of each other's medicine. That policy made us all likely better candidates for teaching in institutions calling their departments "German Language & Literature."

When I received the PhD in early 1958, jobs teaching German were much easier to come by than now, so I quickly landed one at Mt. Holyoke. I was tempted but did not mention in my application that I was beginning to write poems seriously in German. I knew I had to author some scholarly articles, and a couple helped land me my next job teaching at Harvard, where during the next two years I got enough courage to let a few people know of my poems in German. I owe Michael Mann, Egon Schwarz, and Melitta Gerhard especially for encouraging me to take them even more seriously.

How Michael Mann came to work on a PhD in German at Harvard, after abandoning a career as a violist and first being turned down for PhD work at Columbia, is a story someone should pursue. But there he was in a literature course I began teaching, raising a hand from the back row when I called the roll the first day. Egon Schwarz was a more senior faculty member, who took a warm interest in junior faculty. Along with Michael, as I recall, Egon helped organize something of a literary salon, to which I was eventually invited to present some of my poems and take questions I was barely able to answer. I simply didn't understand what I was up to, exactly. Melitta Gerhard, whose work on Stefan George was singularly inspiring, also invited me along with others from the German community at Harvard, to share our work at her place.

Early on in these friendships, which to my great benefit and gratitude lasted till the end of their lives, they commented pointedly on whatever I shared. At times, one or another suggested I try the more constrained German texts in English. Previously, I had sometimes started writing in one language, only to find myself seeing and/or hearing the next line in the other so that hybrids emerged. Thanks to this particular suggestion, as soon as I finished a text in one language I translated it into the other; and a majority of the poems I've published in both languages knew some life at one point in both, while a minority are as exact a translation of each as I could forge. As I write now, many years later, in my mind's eye I often see whatever language I'm using immediately in the other. Dreams also come at times in one tongue, only to continue in the other. There are interesting studies of how bilinguals switch between languages, which I've dipped into; and the whole field of multilingualism in general is attracting more and more researchers. However, I want to stay within the parameters of my own experience for now.

Though I had a three-year contract at Harvard, I left after two because the handwriting on the wall was clear: only one or two of our number would be kept, promoted to assistant professor; and the rest of us knew who they'd be. Jobs in German were still relatively numerous. When I interviewed for one at Duke and one at Oberlin, both resulted in offers. Having wondered to this day what my life would have been like had I taken the position at Duke, with an opportunity to be mentored by the chair, Herman Salinger, I continue to read his superb translations of German poetry. Given how warmly he hosted my wife and me, I still pine at times for what life there might have afforded us and how his expertise as a translator and poet might have affected my development.

At first, life in the German Department at Oberlin was

collegial if not entirely harmonious. John Kurtz, the chairman and an elder statesman, was adept at keeping tensions to a minimum, and he was open to initiatives, if firm about the central mission. Allowed to take an early turn directing the German summer session in Vienna, I was encouraged to arrange side-trips to visit German poets with whom I'd begun developing contacts. Three, Karl Krolow, Günter Eich, and Kuno Raeber not only read to us from their work in their home settings; they encouraged us to try to translate anything that "spoke to us," thus planting a fertile seed. Soon I was supervising translation projects as well as trying my own hand at versions, some of which I sent off to the poets we'd met. On occasion, they returned them with comments. Thus channels were opened that only shut when they died. With permission to translate and such critical commentary from the poets themselves, I—and some students as well—had a platform on which to build working relationships with many another writer since.

Thanks to Chairman Kurtz's efforts, the Max Kade Foundation had for some time funded some of our German House's programs. Working even more magic with his genial ways, John convinced the foundation to establish The Max Kade Writer-in-Residence position at Oberlin, which has brought a writer to Oberlin every year since 1967: Kuno Raeber, for whom I lobbied, became the first and replaced me when I left on sabbatical. Though I went off to Zurich to write a book I was under contract to write for the Twayne Series, on C. F. Meyer, the 19th-century Swiss writer I wrote my dissertation on, I soon questioned the ways Twayne wanted such a biography structured. Meanwhile, I was writing more and more poems in German, which were stealing time from my obligation to finish the Meyer tome. One way out of the dilemma occurred to me: just translate the German texts into what would be my first attempts to write seriously in English, hoping such activity would not cost as much energy, not to mention brain power, so the Meyer book could be front and center. I sensed writing in German was sapping my strength altogether. At the same time, I began questioning, as I have written elsewhere,[2] my mission as a teacher. Of what? German? German language and/ or German literature? Translation? Creative Writing in German? In English, perhaps?! — all courses I was embarked on teaching, or planning to join with colleagues to teach, at Oberlin. Now convinced I risked losing my moorings the more I tried writing in German, I came to something of a full stop. My back went out lifting a toothbrush one morning. Grudgingly acknowledging that stress was now in charge of my body's habits, I took myself off to a Swiss specialist, who applied the latest electrical machinery to calm my aching back, which also restored some mental balance. A writer himself, he took an interest in my quandary, suggesting I put a lid on my German "concoctions" — his very word — by sending out a batch to the best journal I knew of; and meanwhile just put the whole "caboodle" into a something like a manuscript with a "catchy" title, asking around about possible publishers.

When the batch was snatched up just a few weeks later by *Neue deutsche Hefte*, edited by Joachim Günter out of his domicile in Berlin, who found it "curious" they were my first German publication, my right brain lit up: I mentioned in passing having a manuscript to circulate; and in some back and forth paid tribute to Krolow's and Eich's poetry, among others that was boosting me along. Günter not only invited me to visit when next in Berlin, he suggested a small press that might be interested; AND why not write Krolow, say, to see if he'd write something of a foreword or afterword, as that would likely get me read by publishers … Stealing time from eking out a few more pages of the Meyer book, I managed to put together *Kein Trinkwasser*, into which I funneled most every poem in German I'd written, including

---

2 See "Prologue" (in *First & Last Words: Memoir & Stories* — Pinyon Publishing, 2017)

a number based on life in Zurich. I still can't quite believe Krolow agreed to write an afterword, and not long afterward, Atelier Verlag/Andernach, the press Günter had recommended, accepted it. I drank my way through a bottle of Dole, the Swiss wine my wife and I had taken to stocking by the case. Now possessed, I boxed away the Meyer pages, and in something of a stupor collected all the texts I'd been writing in English alongside the German poems—some quarter of which were variations or direct translations—into a "twin" volume, which was accepted by Vanderbilt U. Press. Both appeared in 1969, a year after we returned from Zurich. In my euphoria, I'd momentarily forgotten about the now suspended Meyer project.

The sabbatical soon about to end, I realized I'd have a lot of explaining to do: to Twayne for breaking the contract; to President Robert Carr and the Oberlin Faculty Council who had granted me "Research Status" for the whole year; and to the German Department, who fully expected me to return with at least a draft of the Meyer book. Dark thoughts of facing possible dismissal clouded our return. Chairman Kurtz said softly but firmly: "I'm greatly disappointed. You were hired to be a teacher and a scholar, not a poet." I had at least the good sense not to blurt out that I'd meanwhile had two books of poems accepted.

If President Carr hadn't come to my rescue, I'd likely not be writing this now. "These things happen," he began; and not only was he looking forward to signed copies of the poetry books, he took note of the extra attention colleagues in English and Romance Languages and I had been devoting to students interested in writing their own poems—we'd conducted open workshops on our own time, even co-taught several January-term writing and translation workshops. His words gave me the courage to face some real hostility from my German Department colleagues, emboldening me as well to incorporate poem-writing assignments in German.

As anyone in academia knows, all departments have interpersonal issues. Aside from Oberlin's twinning of German and Russian, with all the problems such a union can propagate, the German side was fraught with its own sometimes high dramas, which I'll leave for the porch in Purgatory; except to say that in addition to the above-mentioned "troubles," they eventually led to our "divorce"—alas the settlement cost the German Department my position when I was permitted to leave with tenure, which galled some faculty. With support from a new administration, under the visionary—some would say problematic—leadership of President Robert Fuller, colleagues and I began to build what has since become The Creative Writing Program. With its own major, it thrives to this day, continuing to attract large numbers of students.

The freelance translation workshops we'd conducted on our own time, during which we urged students to write companion poems of their own—if studying/translating a poem by Raeber about a certain saint, write about a saint of your choosing!—showed over and over that whatever students next wrote on their own was an improvement over previous work. That "evidence" convinced us to require students to take an intro translation course—the nature of which to be developed over time—before allowing students to begin the intro writing course. Time for an aside: an exciting prospective student, whose high school portfolio had been overpraised but under-cherished, threw something of a tantrum when she arrived in the fall to learn she'd have to take the translation class before starting on the path to a creative writing major. Claiming I'd promised she could immediately take intro writing, she even enlisted her lawyer-father's help in taking her case to the president.

The tears long dried up, her father having returned home with a better understanding of our pedagogical thinking, she grew into one of our many accomplished poets, who's still making her mark. Some time ago, she not only wrote a moving apology, the beautiful lamp she gifted me with still lights my desk. Alas, lacking enough faculty to teach translation to growing numbers of applicants, along with a number of other considerations impacting the evolving structure of the writing program, we reluctantly made translation workshop a second-level optional course, still in the curriculum many years later.

At its core, the translation workshop provides young writers a chance to practice fundamentals while working on masterpieces from other languages; and what better source to tap than the European poets colleagues and I were starting to work with?' Hence poems by Aichinger, Celan, Eich, Holub, Krolow, Pedretti, Raboni, Raeber, Sorescu, Vaiciunaite and others soon became central subject matter, while students more interested in theoretical issues were given outside reading suggestions, e.g. George Steiner's monumental *After Babel.*

1969 also saw the founding of *Field,* which as I write is closing in on its 100th issue. Its illustrious history itself is a large subject for another time. As a co-founder, I want to call attention to its long-standing interest in fostering translations from the very first issue onward. The flow of translation submissions eventually led to our starting a Translation Series in 1978 in tandem with the magazine. To many people's surprise, our first two books won the PEN Translation Award: Charles Wright's Montale translations, *The Storm*; and Charles Simic's Vasko Popa tome, *Homage to the Lame Wolf.* Some twenty-five volumes comprise the series so far, which is likely to continue for the life of Oberlin College Press, subsequently established to add a prize for original poetry among other ventures.

While the initial policy, which holds till today, does not permit editors to publish their own poems in any of the press's publications, translations are an exception. Having had a hand in three volumes in the series — Eich, Krolow, Sorescu — I confess there's no other writing project I've undertaken that has given me more pleasure, nor I dare say contributed more to my own development, while at the same time deepening collaborative relationships with other writers over the years I've been privileged to be a part of the press's doings.

Having written elsewhere of working on Eich, Krolow, and Holub under their supervision — at times in collaboration with David Young, David Walker, and Dana Hábová, I want to expand on a note on teaching translation that emanated from a visit to Bucharest to work with Marin Sorescu.[3] Some backstory's in order: thanks to Adriana Varga, a student at Oberlin who was born in Romania, I was able to unlock a few more secrets to Sorescu's words and ways than I could paging around in an old Romanian dictionary buried in storage in the college library; enough to know I had to travel to Bucharest if I wanted to get "serious," assuming Sorescu would be willing to receive me. To set the bureaucratic wheels in motion, I wrote him in care of his British publisher — it appeared as if he couldn't get anything published for some time in Romania. Not only did he write back, he invited me to Bucharest a.s.a.p. because "you never know what might happen a millisecond from now" — a vintage MS reply, I'd later learn. Addressing my concern about whether or not, working together, we'd know enough of each other's tongue to find our way to viable literals, from which to arrive eventually at deep-running versions, he said his dear friend Gabriela Dragnea would make us a trio. "Her English may even be better than yours …" He ended the letter with a comical little self-portrait.

Arranging for me to stay at a hotel around the corner, he urged me to order the deluxe breakfast, which included pineapple

---

3   See "On Teaching Translation at the Introductory Level" (*Translation Review*, Number 63, 2002); parts have been revised and expanded for this article.

juice "straight from America," to which he was addicted. Moments after he opened the door to his cozy house, he asked how I liked the juice! I didn't have the heart to tell him a waiter confessed it was watered down from Roundy's tins of crushed pineapple, which had sat for years in a storeroom rusting away. The waiter had to use a hammer to pound a screwdriver through the tops. When I let that slip during dinner—Virginia Sorescu's stew to "live for"—Sorescu chided me: "Assuming you've read my poems at all, surely you know that's exactly the sort of story I love to hear!" Later that first night, we started right in on the poems Adriana and I'd begun to work through back in Oberlin. If all went well, I slipped in that we might have ourselves a volume for the Field Translation Series. I'd forgotten I'd sent him some of the series, so was surprised when he lit up, "My good friend Seamus Heaney will not say 'no' to providing an introduction, if we live that long!"

Gabriela Dragnea joined us for coffee and sweets. From the moment she spoke, I *knew* Gabriela had to be brought aboard as co-translator, along with Adriana Varga. Huddling around the table we discussed choices, especially establishing the right voice for the poems, till nearby church bells tolled midnight. Agreeing to continue "negotiations" over a working lunch the next day—begging Virginia Sorescu to keep it simple!—we said our goodbyes, at which point Sorescu surprised Gabriela and me with red-ink drawings he'd made of our "mugs" to post in our local P.O., he joked. He'd been drawing us all along underneath the table, his sketchpad always at the ready. On the way out, when I admired a painting in the hall, he allowed as how it was his pitiful early work. Another aside's in order: he stripped it from its frame and rolled it into a tube he gave me on the way to the airport when I left. At customs, I was immediately surrounded by machine-gun-toting soldiers, forcefully escorted to a dimly lit back room, and told in broken, ugly English I'd be charged with stealing Romanian folk art! Hours after missing my plane, a lawyer "generously provided free of charge by the Ceausescu government" finally contacted Sorescu, who they hoped would be a State's witness. He wrote me later he'd had to hold back a roar! He was himself a writer who had to watch his step and quickly provided a sworn statement: a) the painting was his original artwork; b) he had "freely" given it to me. That wasn't quite that: I was "relieved" of $100 of traveler's checks and told any future visits would require a special visa. Exchanging joking postcards for some time afterward, Sorescu and I agreed there could be no more fitting image for the cover of *Hands Behind My Back: Selected Poems of Marin Sorescu* — which the Field Translation Series has long kept in print — than his "infamous" painting.

Supervised by Marin, Gabriela and I worked feverishly during my stay with time off only for a few excursions, chiefly to give me a sense of the "landscape of the poems." There would be much more to do once I returned and filled Adriana in on matters, but a day or so before departing I could see we had enough for a solid volume so we all relaxed by way of finding out more of one another's lives. Virginia joined us with some apricot brandy to ease us into goodbyes, and Marin had the last word: "Let's better tell a few jokes now, drink a little more brandy, but definitely not to Ceausescu's health, and call it a night," he whispered.

When I retired in 1997, I'd taught for forty years altogether — German language and literature for the first twenty, and poetry and playwriting, nonfiction and translation the last twenty. Having resigned as an editor from *Field* and Oberlin College Press as well, I vowed that the only subject anyone could get me unretired to teach, anywhere, would be translation. So there we were, a class of some twenty-five students who'd chosen to study translation as one of several writing program options, and I, getting more and more comfortable over the first week of classes, in Rice Hall that sunny morning on 9/11/2001. The day after, a third of the class was missing — we soon learned they were either New Yorkers or had family and friends from the city. A few would return in a few days, some not at all. We devoted a class to airing fears, finally deciding unanimously to follow the syllabus down into all its particulars, which I'll post in a moment. First let me say that to this day I still hear on occasion from one or another member; in the words of one, that "thanks to being able to share in other writers' lives so intimately by way of translating their holy words," she could go on living her own no matter the darkening ahead.

In conclusion, here are some things I've tried while trying to teach this marvelous subject for over forty years, because Sorescu is no longer alive to warn me off as he once did when I invited him to Oberlin to teach his poems by way of a translation workshop. "Hah, let's better have another swig," he grunted, passing me the brandy bottle.

Sparing the reader a full account of all the various ingredients I've used, including requisite injunctions, exhortations, and anecdotes to leaven the batter, here's something of a list of the basic ones for what has more or less proved to be a reliable recipe. Incidentally, some five hundred students have eaten thereof, a number of whom have gone on to become fellow bakers: of the more than four hundred books — the list continues to lengthen! — Diane Vreuls and I share from former students, fully forty are volumes of translations, prize winners among them to boot. So don your aprons, in case you're of a mind to start teaching translation, or even just practicing yourself alongside other writing projects. If you've already been teaching translation, so much the better! You should find opportunities to disagree, perhaps quite strongly. I sure hope so!

While theory's useful, resist the urge, at first anyway, as Seamus Heaney once cautioned at Oberlin, to deconstruct rather than to construct. In other words, pay some heed to the many, often diverging views about the nature and substance of the craft, by assigning, say, collateral reading ranging from Steiner's *After Babel* at one end of the spectrum, to Bly's *The Eight Stages of Translation* (which I'd keep in print forever if I were the publisher). A good way to do so is put a substantial bibliography on reserve reading, allowing students to choose whatever appeals, even require them to read around a few hours weekly in this critical literature, log responses in a journal to what engages them; even provide some opportunity in class for sharing these entries, entertaining comments and the like. At mid-term, ask for some samples of these reading notes, but otherwise let theory aspects go at the introductory level, till students have gotten "down and dirty" ferreting along from word to word, if not phoneme to phoneme, in the furrows. Later, perhaps much later after amassing a body of translations, one may argue with "experts" by way of developing one's own essential aesthetic and methodology.

Now for the main elements to the syllabus:

I. The Exercise Portfolio

Over the first two thirds of the semester, line up a series of presentations — say 6-8, one a week, I'd recommend — in whatever languages/literatures you can persuade colleagues, or visitors from far afield, if you're lucky foreign writers otherwise invited to campus, or even just friends in the landscape to challenge your class. With a decent budget (good luck these days!), invite visitors to offer a master-class of their own making beyond presenting an assignment, as well as a reading of their work as translators and writers — such additional interactions will enhance the students' stimulation. A typical line-up of presenters/guests in my workshop highlighted languages like Chinese, Japanese, French, Spanish, Turkish, and Vietnamese; made possible by having in town people like David Young and Jiann Lin to present

Du Mu; Ana Cara, who brought her friend Borges to Oberlin some years ago and has worked on his milongas; Güneli Gün, the Turkish-American writer and award-winning translator; Janice Zinser to present Ponge; and Bruce Weigl, the estimable poet, translator, memoirist, to present current Vietnamese poetry along with daughter Hanh. In addition to any remarks they wish to offer about the craft, the language and literature surrounding the writers they introduce us to, including any "tips" from their own ways of working, guests are asked to provide us with bare-bones literals of the text(s) they want us to translate, walking us through the literals, taking questions and comments in the process. Bringing hitherto untranslated material, I strongly urge them, adds considerable excitement and raises the energy level. Other translators' versions crowd beginners, who give up more easily when confronted with published results. Such comparisons might be instructive and helpful later. The initial focus should be on helping students discover their own resources, tease them out of hiding. Fairly brief texts, mainly poems or short prose, bring out the best in beginners as well, not to mention texts guests really love, have struggled with themselves: nothing like "we're in this together" to promote an enterprising spirit. Though I beg guests for their own solutions, I only share them with the class after they've finished assembling their final exercise portfolio.

One other note: since I'm fluent in German I like to take a turn presenting texts I'm working on at the moment. Beginning the parade of presentations, I spend some time reviewing what I call the manners and morals of translating anyone's work from anywhere, including securing rights to do so if one gets more serious about showing versions outside the class, especially if hoping to publish them. Inasmuch as foreign writers in my experience are often delighted knowing anyone's interested in introducing their work in (American!) English, I urge contacting writers one wants to work on, even if the translator considers herself a rank beginner. A number of former students have established lifelong relationships with writers they first worked on in these workshops. Notice that I've been talking about working with living writers. Of course, there are mountains of material in the world's languages that have yet to see their way into English. However, the principles of working with texts whose authors are dead and gone are in some instances quite different from what faces working with living writers. In short, beginners seem to grow more having a relationship with another living soul, or so I've found. This is perhaps the moment to put aside for more discussion later the question of how fluent one ought to be to "dance the dance": Pound I dimly recall is said to have said, perhaps to Eliot, that it takes two to "tango," one who knows the language into which, the other the language from which … The other overarching aspect to all this is: Can anyone with zero knowledge of the to-be-translated tongue ever hope to translate from it, even provided with supple literals, the deepest linguistic knowledge, as well as the original author's input? This may be apocryphal but I believe a writer of some Asian language said he'd rather have W. S. Merwin translate his work, even if he didn't know a word, than any other writer of English. Guess why!

Some logistics: if you have two 75-minute classes weekly, say Tuesday and Thursday, schedule guests for Thursday so students will have the weekend to work on their initial drafts. Say there are 21 students and 7 exercise-presentations. Ask 3 students to volunteer each time to put their solutions on a worksheet, each having in turn 25 minutes to read her version, talk about her approach, frustrations, and let us hope delights, then take questions and comments. Encourage the class to leave comments for the presenters to collect that could not come up because of time constraints. Encourage students as well to use, in revising, anyone else's solution they regard as superior, footnoting the borrowing, briefly saying why it was "lifted." I myself enter class discussions as little as possible so students can forge closer partnerships among themselves—via in-class exchanges and sharing written comments—that might carry over into joint projects at a later date. Introduce your own comments gingerly, e.g. "You might try…"; "I'm just one reader, so…"; and sometimes, "Please see me if my comments aren't clear or, worse, going down well!" Everyone who's ever taught knows how critical it is to sense what students can hear as well as cannot hear—particularly beginners.

A beneficial parallel assignment to the weekly exercises: require students to try their hand at what I call "companion pieces," inspired let us hope by engaging the foreign texts. Don't grade these pieces! Do review them carefully. Many students report writing these companion texts raised their sights and deepened their insights, often resulting in their strongest work from then on. Hardly surprising: working on masterpieces will usually make a difference in how one goes about one's own work.

These are only guidelines and I happily confess some guests have found other, equally productive ways to engage their students. One instructive byproduct that bears mentioning when guests introduce hitherto untranslated texts: responding with your strongest instincts sometimes results in "misses," even misrepresentations or downright "messes"; but equally often with yeasty possibilities, so to foster an initial, pull-out-all-stops approach, I recount what Miroslav Holub said when initially I showed him some mangled attempts to come to grips with his remarkable poems. Pointing to one egregious mistranslation, that night in Prague, he slapped his thigh and snorted, "I like it, we keep it!" When said poem was eventually allowed to appear in Czech, there was my "mistake"!

Okay, all your guests have come and gone, and mid-term's upon you. So here's what I look for in the exercise portfolio due at that point: two versions of each piece guests have left us to work on — an early attempt and a final-for-now version; five journal entries of responses to a range of reading in the material on reserve; one entry on a critical source students locate on their own beyond the course's bibliography; a companion piece to each translation; and a brief intro statement, say 3-5 pages, under this rubric: "Some Things I've Learned on the Way to These Translations."

II. The Final-Exercise Portfolio

Early in the course, I announce that for the final project, which will occupy us after the exercises are completed, students will be expected to work together in small groups — three's a good number to break a tie vote, I joke; two's a minimum. No one may work alone, even with outside help or personal expertise, for reasons I challenge students to imagine. To facilitate matching up well in teams, at the first meeting I ask students to list "languages and literatures I'm fluent in"; "languages and literatures I'd be interested in working on, even with little or no expertise." I tell the tale of Christine Molinari, of deep Italian roots, who nonetheless "confessed" that for unknown reasons she'd like to pursue a project in Hungarian. Long story short: she eventually mastered Hungarian so well that once she moved to Budapest she met the great poet Sándor Csoóri, who later told me he couldn't hope for a better translator than Christine!

The list of what languages students know, along with level of expertise, interests in other tongues, a la Christine, gives them ideas for working with others who share similar interests. In addition, students sometimes mention specific writers they'd like to entice others to work on with them: writers they may have met studying abroad; even writers in their family from other lands. Enlarging the circle, there are always foreign students on campus to turn to for ideas and expertise, as well as alumni living abroad who are usually eager to help. So, with the major mission in mind — to identify a writer or writers whose work cries out for translation, and whom students want to translate with all their heart and soul — groups embark on a journey to narrow their specific choices of which texts to collaborate on, divvying up responsibilities — let students decide who does what and how much on the way to preparing a seminar-style report to the class in the remaining sessions. Supplying us with samples of their translations in advance, they initiate the class discussion by highlighting: why this writer, why this work? Other discussion topics include how they approached the material, their ways with particular solutions, even their fights! The session concludes with questions and comments from the class, which often prove helpful to the presenters as they prepare a final manuscript. Each student includes a personal statement, delineating her or his specific contributions to the project. Ending the course with a class reading, students read a favorite translation as well as the companion piece written as a response.

Born in Wisconsin, **STUART FRIEBERT** spent an undergraduate year in Germany as one of the first U.S. exchange students after WW II, after which he finished a BA at Wisconsin State College/Milwaukee and took an MA and a PhD at U. Wisconsin/Madison in German Language & Literature. He began teaching at Mt. Holyoke College, then at Harvard, and finally settled at Oberlin College, where he taught German and founded and directed Oberlin's Creative Writing Program until retiring in 1997. Along the way, he co-founded *Field* Magazine, the Field Translation Series, and Oberlin College Press.

Friebert has published fifteen books of poems (including volumes in German), sixteen volumes of translations, anthologies, and more recently prose (stories, memoir pieces, and critical essays). He has held an N.E.A. Fellowship in poetry and received numerous awards for poems and translations, including the Four Way Book Award for *Funeral Pie* and the Ohioana Book Award for *Floating Heart*.

Models of the Universe: An Anthology of the Prose Poem
  (with David Young)

TRANSLATIONS

Günter Eich: Valuable Nail: Selected Poems
  (with David Walker and David Young)

Sylva Fischerová: The Swing in the Middle of Chaos: Selected Poems
  (with the author)

Sylva Fischerová: Stomach of the Soul: Selected Poems
  (with the author and A. J. Hauner)

Ute von Funcke: Between Question & Answer: Selected Poems

Ute von Funcke: Shadow of Shadows: Selected Poems

Miroslav Holub: Sagittal Section: Selected Poems
  (with Dana Hábová)

Karl Krolow: On Account Of: Selected Poems

Karl Krolow: Puppets in the Wind: Selected Poems

Karl Krolow: What'll We Do With This Life?: Selected Poems

Giovanni Raboni: The Coldest Year of Grace: Selected Poems
  (with Vinio Rossi)

Kuno Raeber: Be Quiet: Selected Poems

Kuno Raeber: Votives: Selected Poems
  (with Christiane Wyrwa)

Kuno Raeber: Watch Out: Selected Poems

Elisabeth Schmeidel: Scant Hours: Selected Poems

Marin Sorescu: Hands Behind My Back: Selected Poems
  (with Gabriela Dragnea and Adriana Varga)

Judita Vaičiūnaitė: Fire, Put Out By Fire: Selected Poems
  (with Viktoria Skrupskelis)

TEXTBOOK

Max Frisch: Als der Krieg zu Ende war